Hengist, King of Kent by Thomas Middleton

or, The Mayor of Quinborough

For this play about post-Roman Britain, Middleton drew upon Fabyan's Chronicle of 1559 and Holinshed's History of England of 1587.

Thomas Middleton was born in London in April 1580 and baptised on 18th April.

Middleton was aged only five when his father died. His mother remarried but this unfortunately fell apart into a fifteen year legal dispute regarding the inheritance due Thomas and his younger sister.

By the time he left Oxford, at the turn of the Century, Middleton had and published Microcynicon: Six Snarling Satirese which was denounced by the Archbishop of Canterbury and publicly burned.

In the early years of the 17th century, Middleton wrote topical pamphlets. One – Penniless Parliament of Threadbare Poets was reprinted several times and the subject of a parliamentary inquiry.

These early years writing plays continued to attract controversy. His writing partnership with Thomas Dekker brought him into conflict with Ben Jonson and George Chapman in the so-called War of the Theatres.

His finest work with Dekker was undoubtedly The Roaring Girl, a biography of the notorious Mary Frith.

In the 1610s, Middleton began another playwriting partnership, this time with the actor William Rowley, producing another slew of plays including Wit at Several Weapons and A Fair Quarrel.

The ever adaptable Middleton seemed at ease working with others or by himself. His solo writing credits include the comic masterpiece, A Chaste Maid in Cheapside, in 1613.

In 1620 he was officially appointed as chronologer of the City of London, a post he held until his death.

The 1620s saw the production of his and Rowley's tragedy, and continual favourite, The Changeling, and of several other tragicomedies.

However in 1624, he reached a peak of notoriety when his dramatic allegory A Game at Chess was staged by the King's Men. Though Middleton's approach was strongly patriotic, the Privy Council silenced the play after only nine performances at the Globe theatre, having received a complaint from the Spanish ambassador.

What happened next is a mystery. It is the last play recorded as having being written by Middleton.

Thomas Middleton died at his home at Newington Butts in Southwark in the summer of 1627, and was buried on July 4th, in St Mary's churchyard which today survives as a public park in Elephant and Castle.

Index of Contents

Dramatis Personae
Chorus: RAYNULPH, Monk of Chester
CONSTANTIUS, King of the Britons
VORTIGER
HENGIST, King of Kent
AURELIUS and UTHER, Brothers to Constantius
HORSUS
DEVONSHIRE and STAFFORD, two Lords
LUPUS and GERMANUS, two Monks
CASTIZA, Daughter to Devonshire

ROXENA, Daughter to Hengist
Two LADIES
SIMON, a tanner, Mayor of Quinborough
OLIVER, a fustian weaver
Three GRAZIERS
GLOVER
BARBER
TAILOR
FELLMONGER
BUTTONMONGER
Honeysuckle, a BRAZIER
Petitioners
GENTLEMEN
AMINADAB, a clerk
FOOTMAN
SAXONS, soldiers, captain, guard, and officers
MONKS
Villains
Vortimer, son of Vortiger
British Lords
CHEATERS, including a CLOWN

Enter **RAYNULPH**, a monk, the presenter.

RAYNULPH
What Raynulph monk of Chester can
Raise from his Polychronicon,
That raises him as works do men
To see light so long parted with again,
That best may please this round, fair ring
With sparkling judgments circled in
I shall produce; if all my powers
Can win the grace of two poor hours,
Well a-paid I go to rest.
Ancient stories have been best.
Fashions that are now call'd new
Have been worn by more than you;
Elder times have us'd the same,
Though these new ones get the name:
So in story what's now told
That takes not part with days of old?
Then to prove time's mutual glory
Join new time's love to old time's story.

[Exit.

SCENE I - Before a Monastery

Shout. Enter **VORTIGER**.

VORTIGER
Will that wide-throated beast, the multitude,
Never lin bellowing? Courtiers are ill-advis'd
When they first make such monsters.
How near was I to a sceptre and a crown!
Fair power was e'en upon me; my desires
Were tasting glory till this forked rabble
With their infectious acclamations
Poisoned my fortune. They will here have none
As long as Constantine's three sons survive,
As if vassals knew not how to obey
But in that line, like their professions
That all their lifetime hammer out one way,
Beaten into their pates with seven years' bondage.
Well, though I rise not king, I'll seek the means
To grow as close to one as policy can,
And choke their expectations.

[Enter **DEVONSHIRE, STAFFORD**.

Now, good lords,
In whose kind loves and wishes I am built
As high as human dignity can aspire,
Are yet those trunks that have no other souls
But noise and ignorance something more quiet?

DEVONSHIRE
Nor are they like to be for ought we gather.
Their wills are up still: nothing will appease 'em;
Good speeches are but cast away upon 'em.

VORTIGER
Then, since necessity and fate withstand me,
I'll strive to enter at a straighter passage.
Your sudden aids and counsels, good my lords.

STAFFORD
They're ours no longer than they do you service.

[Music. Enter certain **MONKS** including **LUPUS** and **GERMANUS**, **CONSTANTIUS** being one, singing as at precession, and **AURELIUS** and **UTHER**. Song.

MONKS
Boast not of high birth or blood;
To be great is to be good.
Holy and religious things,
Those are vestures fit for kings;
By how much man in fame shines clearer,
He to heaven should draw the nearer,
He deserving best of praises
Whom virtue raises.
It is not state, it is not birth;
The way to heaven is grace on earth.
Sing to the temple him so holy
Sin may blush to think on folly.

VORTIGER
Vessels of sanctity, be pleas'd a while
To give attention to the public peace,
Wherein heaven is serv'd too, though not so purely:
Constantius, eldest son of Constantine,
We here seize on thee for the general good,
And in thy right of birth.

CONSTANTIUS
On me! For what, lords?

VORTIGER
The kingdom's government.

CONSTANTIUS
Oh, powers of blessedness!
Keep me from growing downwards into earth again;
I hope I am further on my way than so.
[To **MONKS**] Set forward.

VORTIGER
You must not.

CONSTANTIUS
How!

VORTIGER
I know your wisdom
Will light upon a way to pardon us
When you shall read in every Briton's brow
The urg'd necessity of the times.

CONSTANTIUS
What necessity
Can be i' th' world but prayer and repentance?
And that business I am about.

[Shout.

VORTIGER
Hark, afar off still!
We lose and hazard much. Holy Germanus
And reverend Lupus, with all expedition
Set the crown on him.

CONSTANTIUS
No such mark of fortune
Comes near my head.

VORTIGER
My lord, we are forc'd to rule you.

CONSTANTIUS
Dare you receive heaven's light in at your eyelids
And offer violence to religion? Take heed,
The very beam let in to comfort you
May be the fire to burn you; on these knees,
Hardened with zealous prayers, I entreat you
Bring not my cares into the world again.
Think with how much unwillingness and anguish
A glorified soul parted from the body
Would to that loathsome gaol return again;
With such great pain a well subdued affection
Reenters worldly business.

VORTIGER
Good my lord,
I know you cannot lodge so many virtues,
But patience must be one. As low as earth
We beg the freeness of your own consent,
Which else must be constrain'd, and time it were
Either agreed or forc'd. Speak, good my lord,
For you bind up more sin in this delay
Than thousand prayers can absolve again.

CONSTANTIUS
Were 't but my death, you should not kneel so long for't.

VORTIGER

'Twill be the death of millions if you rise not,
And that betimes too. Lend your helps, my lords,
For fear all come too late.

CONSTANTIUS
This is a cruelty
That peaceful man did never suffer yet,
To make me die again that was once dead,
And begin all that ended long before.
Hold, Lupus and Germanus, you are lights
Of holiness and religion. Can you offer
The thing that is not lawful? Stand not I
Clear from all temporal charge by my profession?

GERMANUS
Not when a time so violent calls upon you.
Who's born a prince is born for general peace,
Not his own only; heaven will look for him
In others' business and require him there.
What is in you religious must be shown
In saving many more souls than your own.

CONSTANTIUS
Did not great Constantine, our noble father,
Deem me unfit for government and rule,
And therefore pressed me into this profession,
Which I have held strict and love it above glory?
Nor is there want in me; yourselves can witness
Heaven has provided largely for your peace
And bless'd you with the lives of my two brothers:
Fix your obedience there, leave me a servant.

VORTIGER [To **LUPUS** and **GERMANUS**]
You may even at this instant.

[**CONSTANTIUS** is crowned.

CONSTANTIUS
Oh, this cruelty!

ALL
Long live Constantius, son of Constantine, King of the Britons!

[Flourish.

AURELIUS
They have chang'd their tune already.

CONSTANTIUS

I feel want
And extreme poverty of joy within me:
The peace I had is parted 'mongst rude men;
To keep them quiet I have lost it all.
What can the kingdom gain by my undoing?
That riches is not bless'd, though it be mighty,
That's purchas'd with the spoil of any man,
Nor can the peace so filch'd ever thrive with 'em;
And if't be worthily held sacrilege
To rob a temple, 'tis no less offence
To ravish meditations from a soul,
The consecrated altar in a man,
And all their hopes will be beguil'd in me.
I know no more the way to temporal rule
Than he that's born and has his years to him
In a rough desert; well may the weight kill me,
And that's the fairest good I look for from't.

VORTIGER

Not so, great king: here stoops a faithful servant
Would sooner perish under it with cheerfulness
Than your meek soul should feel oppression
Of ruder cares; such common, coarse employments
Cast upon me your subject, upon Vortiger.
I see you are not made for noise and pains,
Clamours of suitors, injuries and redresses,
Millions of rising actions with the sun,
Like laws still ending and yet never done,
Of power to turn a great man to the state
Of his insensible monument with o'erwatching.
To be oppress'd is not required of you, my lord,
But only to be king: the broken sleeps
Let me take from you, sir; the toils and troubles,
All that is burthensome in authority,
Please you lay't on me, and what is glorious
Receive it to your own brightness.

CONSTANTIUS

Worthy Vortiger,
If 'twere not sin to grieve another's patience
With what we cannot tolerate ourselves,
How happy were I in thee and thy charity.
There's nothing makes man feel his miseries
But knowledge only: reason, that is plac'd
For man's director, is his chief afflicter,
For though I cannot bear the weight myself,
I cannot have that barrenness of remorse

To see another groan under my burthen.

VORTIGER [Aside]
I'm quite blown up a conscionable way;
There's even a trick of murdering in some pity.
The death of all my hopes I see already:
There was no other likelihood, for religion
Was never friend of mine yet.

CONSTANTIUS [To **MONKS**]
Holy partners
In strictest abstinence, fastings and vigils,
Cruel necessity has forc'd me from you.
We part I fear forever, but in mind
I will be always here; here let me stay.

DEVONSHIRE
My lord, you know the times.

CONSTANTIUS
Farewell, bless'd souls, I fear I much offend;
He that draws tears from you takes your best friend.

[Flourish.

[Exeunt all but **VORTIGER.**]

VORTIGER
Can this great motion of ambition stand
Like wheels false wrought by an unskillful hand?
Then, time, stand thou too; let no hopes arrive
At their sweet wishfulness till mine set forward.
Would I could stay this existence as I can
Thy glassy counterfeit in hours of sand!
I'd keep thee turn'd down till my wishes rose,
Then we'd both rise together.
What several inclinations are in nature!
How much is he disquieted, and wears royalty
Disdainfully upon him like a curse.
Calls a fair crown the weight of his afflictions,
When here's a soul would sing under the burthen!
Yet well recovered: I will seek all ways
To vex authority from him; I will weary him
As low as the condition of a hound
Before I give him over, and in all
Study what most may discontent his blood,
Making my mask my zeal to th' public good.
Not possible a richer policy

Can have conception in the thought of man.

[Enter three **GRAZIERS**.

FIRST GRAZIER
An honourable life enclose your lordship.

VORTIGER
Now, what are you?

SECOND GRAZIER
Graziers, an't like your lordship.

VORTIGER
So it should seem by your enclosures;
What's your affairs with me?

FIRST GRAZIER
We are your petitioners, my lord.

VORTIGER
What? Depart!
Petitioners to me! Y'have well deserv'd
My grace and friendship, have you not a ruler
After your own election? Hie to court,
Get near and close, be loud and bold enough,
You cannot choose but speed.

[Exit.

SECOND GRAZIER
And that will do't,
We have throats wide enough, we'll put 'em to't.

[Exeunt.

DUMB SHOW I

Music. Dumb show: **FORTUNE** is discovered upon an altar, in her hand a golden round full of lots. Enter **HENGIST** and **HORUS** with others; they draw lots and hang them up with joy: so all depart saving **HENGIST** and **HORUS**, who kneel and embrace each other as partners in one fortune. To them enter **ROXENA**, seeming to take her leave of **HENGIST** her father, but especially privately and warily of **HORUS** her lover; she departs weeping, and **HENGIST** and **HORUS** go to the door and bring in their **SOLDIERS** with drum and colours, and so march forth.

Enter **RAYNULPH**

RAYNULPH
When Germany was overgrown
With sons of peace too thickly sown,
Several guides were chosen then
By destin'd lots to lead out men,
And they whom Fortune here withstands
Must prove their fates in other lands.
On these two captains fell that lot;
But that which must not be forgot,
Was Roxena's cunning grief,
Who from the father like a thief,
Hid her best and truest tears
Which her lustful lover wears,
In many a stol'n and wary kiss
Unseen of father: that maids will do this
Yet highly scorn to be call'd strumpets too,
But what they lack on't I'll be judg'd by you.

[Exit.

SCENE I - A Hall in the Palace

Enter **VORTIGER, FELLMONGER, BUTTONMERGER, BRAZIERS, GRAZIERS**, and other **PETITIONERS**.

VORTIGER
This way his majesty comes.

ALL
Thank your good lordship.

VORTIGER
When you hear yon door open—

FELLMONGER
Very good, my lord.

VORTIGER
Be ready with your several suits; put forward.

FIRST GRAZIER
That's a thing every man does naturally, sir,

That's a suitor, if he mean to speed.

VORTIGER
'Tis well y'are so deep-learn'd; take no denials.

FELLMONGER
No, my good lord.

VORTIGER
Not any, if you love
The prosperity of your suits; you mar all utterly
And overthrow your fruitful hopes forever
If either fifth or sixth, nay, tenth repulse
Fasten upon your bashfulness.

BUTTONMONGER
Say you so, my lord?
We can be troublesome and we list.

VORTIGER
I know't.
[Aside] I felt it but too late in the general sum
Of your rank brotherhood, which now I'll thank you for.
While this vexation is in play, I'll study
To raise a second, then a third to that,
One still to back another. I'll make quietness
As dear and precious to him as night's rest
To a man in suits in law: he shall be glad
To yield up power; if not, it shall be had.

[Exit.

BUTTONMONGER
Hark! I protest my heart was coming upward, I thought the door had open'd.

FIRST GRAZIER
Marry, would it had, sir.

BUTTONMONGER
I have such a treacherous heart of mine own, 'twill throb at the very fall of a farthingale.

FIRST GRAZIER
Not if it fall on the rushes.

BUTTONMONGER
Yes, truly, if there be no light in the room I shall throb presently. The first time it took me my wife was i' th' company; I remember the room was not half so light as this, but I'll be sworn I was a whole hour a-finding on her.

BRAZIER
Byrlady, y'had a long time of throbbing on't then!

BUTTONMONGER
Still I felt men, but I could feel no women; I thought they had been all sunk. I have made a vow for't, I'll never have a meeting by candlelight again.

FIRST GRAZIER
Yes, sir, in lanthorns.

BUTTONMONGER
Yes, sir, in lanthorns, but I'll never trust a naked candle again, take 't on my word.

[Enter **CONSTANTIUS** and two **GENTLEMEN**.

FIRST GRAZIER
Hark there, stand close! It opens now indeed.

BUTTONMONGER
Oh, majesty, what art thou! I'd give any man half my suit to deliver my petition now; 'tis in the behalf of button-makers, and so it seems by my flesh.

CONSTANTIUS [To the **GENTLEMEN**]
Pray do not follow me, unless you do't
To wonder at my garments; there's no cause
I give you why you should. 'Tis shame enough
Methinks for me to look upon myself;
It grieves me that more should: the other weeds
Became me better, but the lords are pleas'd
To force me to wear these; I would not else.
I pray be satisfied, I call'd you not.
Wonder of madness, can you stand so idle
And know that you must die?

FIRST GENTLEMAN
We are all commanded, sir;
Besides it is our duty to your grace
To give attendance.

CONSTANTIUS
What a wild thing's this!
We marvel though you tremble at death's name
When you'll not see the cause why you are cowards.
All our attendances are far too little
On our own selves, yet you'll give me attendance
Who looks to you the whilst, and so you vanish
Strangely and fearfully. For charity's sake,

Make not my presence guilty of your sloth;
Withdraw, young men, and find you honest business.

SECOND GENTLEMAN [Aside to **FIRST GENTLEMAN**]
What hopes have we to rise by following him?
I'll give him over shortly.

FIRST GENTLEMAN [Aside to **SECOND GENTLEMAN**]
He's too nice,
Too holy for young gentlemen to follow
That have good faces and sweet running fortunes.

[Exeunt **GENTLEMEN**.

CONSTANTIUS
Eight hours a day in serious contemplation
Is but a bare allowance, no higher food
To th' soul than bread and water to the body,
And that's but needful then: more would do better.

FIRST GRAZIER
Let's all kneel together; 'twill move pity:
I have been at begging a hundred suits.

[The **PETITIONERS** kneel.

CONSTANTIUS
How happy am I in the sight of you!
Here are religious souls that lose no time.
With what devotion do they kneel to heaven
And seem to check me that am so remiss!
I bring my zeal amongst you, holy men;
If I see any kneel and I sit out,
That hour is not well serv'd, methinks. Strict souls,
You have been of some order in your times?

FIRST GRAZIER
Graziers and braziers some, and this a fellmonger.

BRAZIER
Here's my petition.

BUTTONMONGER
Mine, an't like your grace.

FIRST GRAZIER
Look upon mine, I am the longest suitor:
I was undone seven years ago, my lord.

CONSTANTIUS

I have mock'd my good hopes. Call you these petitions?
Why, there's no form of prayer among 'em all!

BUTTONMONGER

Yes, i' th' bottom there's some half a line
Prays for your majesty if you look on mine.

CONSTANTIUS

Make your request to heaven, not to me.

BUTTONMONGER

'Las, mine's a supplication for brass buttons, sir.

FELLMONGER

There's a great enormity in wool, I beseech your grace consider 't.

FIRST GRAZIER

Pastures rise to twopence an acre, my lord. What will this world come to?

BUTTONMONGER

I do beseech your grace!

FIRST GRAZIER

Good your grace!

CONSTANTIUS

Oh, this is one of my afflictions
That with the crown enclos'd me! I must bear it.

FIRST GRAZIER

Your grace's answer to my supplication!

BRAZIER

To mine, my lord!

CONSTANTIUS

No violent storm lasts ever,
That's all the comfort on't.

FELLMONGER

Your highness' answer!

FIRST GRAZIER

We are almost half undone, the country beggar'd!

BRAZIER

See, see, he points to heaven, as who should say
There's enough there; but 'tis a great way thither.
There's no good to be done here, I see that; we may all spend our mouths like a company of hounds in the chase of a royal deer, and go home and fall to cold mutton bones, when we have done.

BUTTONMONGER
My wife will hang me; that's my destiny.

[Exeunt all but **CONNSTANTIUS**.

CONSTANTIUS
Thanks, heaven, 'tis over; we should never know rightly
The sweetness of a calm but for a tempest.
Here's a wish'd hour for contemplation now,
All still and silent; this is a true kingdom.

[Enter **VORTIGER**.

VORTIGER
My lord.

CONSTANTIUS
Again?

VORTIGER
Alas, this is but early
And gentle to the troops of businesses
That flock about authority, my lord.
You must forthwith settle your mind to marry.

CONSTANTIUS
To marry!

VORTIGER
Suddenly there's no pause given;
The peoples' wills are violent,
And covetous of succession from your loins.

CONSTANTIUS
From me there can come none: a profess'd abstinence
Hath set a virgin seal upon my blood
And alter'd all the course; the heat I have
Is all enclos'd within a zeal to virtue,
And that's not fit for earthly propagation.
Alas, I shall but forfeit all their hopes;
I'm a man made without desires, tell 'em.

VORTIGER

This gives no satisfaction to their wills, my lord:
I prov'd them with such words, but all were fruitless;
Their sturdy voices blew 'em into clouds.
A virgin of the highest subject's blood
They have pick'd out for your embrace, and send her
Bless'd with their general wishes into fruitfulness.

[Enter **CASTIZA**.

See where she comes, my lord.

CONSTANTIUS [Moving aside]
I never felt
Unhappy hand of misery till this touch;
A patience I could find for all but this.

CASTIZA
My lord, your vow'd love ventures me but dangerously.

VORTIGER
'Tis but to strengthen a vexation politicly.

CASTIZA
That's an uncharitable practice, trust me, sir.

VORTIGER
No more of that.

CASTIZA
But say he should affect me, sir,
How should I 'scape him then? I have but one faith, my lord,
And that you have already; our late contract's
A divine witness to't.

VORTIGER
Leave it to me still;
I am not without shifting rooms and helps
For all my projects I commit with you.

[Exit **VORTIGER**.

CASTIZA [Aside]
'Tis an ungodly way to come to honour;
I do not like 't; I love Lord Vortiger,
But not these practices; th'are too uncharitable.

CONSTANTIUS
Are you a virgin?

CASTIZA
Never yet, my lord,
Known to the will of man.

CONSTANTIUS
Oh, blessed creature!
And does too much felicity make you surfeit?
Are you in soul assured there is a state
Prepared for you, for you, a glorious one,
In midst of heaven, now in the state you stand?
And had you rather, after much known misery,
Cares and hard labours, mingled with a curse,
Throng but to th' door and hardly get a place there?
Think, has the world a folly like this madness?
Keep still that holy and immaculate fire,
You chaste lamp of eternity; 'tis a treasure
Too precious for death's moment to partake,
This twinkling of short life. Disdain as much
To let mortality know you as stars
To kiss the pavements; y'have a substance
As excellent as theirs, holding your pureness:
They look upon corruption, as you do,
But are stars still; be you a virgin too.

CASTIZA
I'll never marry, what though my troth be engag'd
To Vortiger. Forsaking all the world
I save it well and do my faith no wrong.
Y'have mightily prevail'd, great virtuous lord;
I'm bound eternally to praise your goodness.

[Enter **VORTIGER** and **FIRST GENTLEMAN**.

I carry thoughts away as pure from man
As ever made a virgin's name immortal.

CONSTANTIUS
I will do that for joy I never did
Nor ever will again.

[He kisses her. Exit **CASTIZA**.

FIRST GENTLEMAN
My lord, he's taken.

VORTIGER
I'm sorry for't; I like not that so well:

They're somewhat too familiar for their time methinks;
This way of kissing is no course to vex him.
Why, I that have a weaker faith and patience
Could endure more than that coming from woman.
Dispatch and bring his answer speedily.

[Exit **VORTIGER**.

FIRST GENTLEMAN
My lord, my gracious lord.

CONSTANTIUS
Beshrew thy heart.

FIRST GENTLEMAN
They all attend your grace.

CONSTANTIUS
I would not have 'em;
'Twould please me better and they'ld all depart
And leave the court to me, or put me out
And take it to theirselves.

FIRST GENTLEMAN
The noon is past, my lord;
Meat's upon the table.

CONSTANTIUS
Meat! Away, get from me;
Thy memory's diseas'd. What saint's eve's this?

FIRST GENTLEMAN
Saint Agatha, I take it.

CONSTANTIUS
Oh, is it so?
I am not worthy to be serv'd before her,
And so return I pray.

FIRST GENTLEMAN
He'll starve the guard and this be suffer'd; if we set court bellies by a monastery clock, he that breaks a fellow's pate now will scarce be able to crack a louse within this twelvemonth.

[Exit.

CONSTANTIUS
Sure 'tis forgetfulness and not man's will
That leads him forth into licentious ways;

He cannot certainly commit such errors
And think upon 'em truly as they are acting.
Why's abstinence ordain'd but for such seasons?

[Enter **VORTIGER**, **DEVONSHIRE** and **STAFFORD**.

VORTIGER
My lord, y'have pleas'd to put us to much pains,
But we confess 'tis portion of our duties.
Will your grace please to walk? Dinner stays for you.

CONSTANTIUS
I have answer'd that already.

VORTIGER
But, my lord,
We must not so yield to you, pardon me:
'Tis for the general good; you must be rul'd, sir.
Your health and life is dearer to us now;
Think where you are, at court: this is no monastery.

CONSTANTIUS
But, sir, my conscience keeps still where it was;
I may not eat this day.

VORTIGER
We have sworn you shall,
And plentifully too; we must preserve you, sir,
Though you'll be wilful: 'tis no slight condition
To be a king.

CONSTANTIUS
Would I were less than man.

VORTIGER
What, will you make the people rise, my lord,
In great despair of your continuance
If you neglect the means that must sustain you?

CONSTANTIUS
I never eat on eves.

VORTIGER
But now you must:
It concerns others' healths that you take food;
Y'have chang'd your life, you well may change your mood.

CONSTANTIUS

This is beyond all cruelty.

VORTIGER
'Tis our care, my lord.

[Exeunt **OMNES**. Music.

SCENE I - A Room in the Palace

Enter **VORTIGER** and **CASTIZA**.

CASTIZA
My lord, I am resolv'd; tempt me no further:
'Tis all to fruitless purpose.

VORTIGER
Are you well?

CASTIZA
Never so perfect in the truth of health
As at this instant.

VORTIGER
Then I doubt my own,
Or that I am not waking.

CASTIZA
Would you were then;
You would praise my resolution.

VORTIGER
This is wondrous.
Are you not mine by contract?

CASTIZA
'Tis most true, my lord,
And I'm better bless'd in't than I look'd for,
In that I am confin'd in faith so strictly:
I'm bound, my lord, to marry none but you;
You'll grant me that, and you I'll never marry.

VORTIGER
It draws into me violence and hazard!
I saw you kiss the king.

CASTIZA

I grant you so, sir.
Where could I take my leave of the world better?
I wrong'd not you in that; you will acknowledge
A king is the best part on't.

VORTIGER

Oh, my passion!

CASTIZA

I see you somewhat yielding to infirmity, sir;
I take my leave.

VORTIGER

Why, 'tis not possible!

CASTIZA

The fault is in your faith; time I was gone
To give it better strengthening.

VORTIGER

Hark you, lady.

CASTIZA

Send your intent to the next monastery;
There you shall find my answer ever after.
And so with my last duty to your lordship,
For whose perfections I will pray as heartily
As for mine own.

[Bows and exit.

VORTIGER

How am I serv'd in this!
I offer a vexation to the king;
He sends it home into my blood with vantage.
I'll put off time no longer. I have wrought him
Into most men's neglect, calling his zeal
A deep pride hallowed over, love of ease
More than devotion or the public benefit,
Which catches many men's beliefs. I am stronger too
In peoples' wishes; their affections point to me.
I lose much time and glory; that redeem'd,
She that now flies returns with joy and wonder:
Greatness and woman's wish never keep asunder.

[Exit.

Hoboys. Dumb show. Enter two **VILLANS**, to them **VORTIGER** seeming to solicit them, gives them gold, then swears them. Exit **VORTIGER**. Enter to them **CONSTANTIUS** in private meditation; they rudely come to him, strike down his book and draw their swords upon him. He fairly spreads his arms and yields to their furies, at which they seem to be overcome with pity, but looking on the gold kill him as he turns his back and hurry away his body. Enter **VORTIGER, DEVONSHIRE, STAFFORD** in private conference; to them enter the murderers presenting the head to **VORTIGER**. He seems to express much sorrow, and before the astonished lords makes officers lay hold on 'em, who offering to come towards **VORTIGER** are commanded to be hurried away as to execution. Then the lords, all seeming respect, crown **VORTIGER**; then bring in **CASTIZA**, who seems to be brought in unwillingly by **DEVONSHIRE** and **STAFFORD** who crown her and then give her to **VORTIGER**, she going forth with him with a kind of constrain'd consent. Then enter **AURELIUS** and **UTHER** the two brothers who much astonished seem to fly for their safety.

Enter **RAYNULPH**

RAYNULPH
When nothing could prevail to tire
The good king's patience, death had hire
In wicked strengths to take his life,
In whom awhile there fell a strife
Of pity and fury, but the gold
Made pity faint and fury bold.
Then to Vortiger they bring
The head of that religious king,
Who, feigning grief, to clear his guilt
Makes the slaughterers' blood be spilt.
Then crown they him and force the maid,
That vow'd a virgin life, to wed.
Such a strength great power extends:
It conquers fathers, kin and friends.
And since fate's pleas'd to change her life,
She proves as holy in a wife.
More to tell were to betray
What deeds in their own tongues must say;
Only this, the good king dead,
The brothers poor in safety fled.

[Exit.

Enter **VORTIGER**, a **GENTLEMAN** meeting him.

GENTLEMAN
My lord!

VORTIGER
I fear thy news will fetch a curse,
It comes with such a violence.

GENTLEMAN
The people are up in arms against you!

VORTIGER
Oh, this dream of glory! I could wish
A sting unto thee; there's no such felt in hell
The fellow but to mine I feel now.
Sweet power, before I can have time to taste thee
Must I forever lose thee? What's the impostume
That swells 'em now?

GENTLEMAN
The murder of Constantius.

[Exit **GENTLEMAN**.

VORTIGER
Ulcers of realms! They hated him alive,
Grew weary of the minute of his reign
Compared with some kings' time, and poisoned him
Often before he died in their black wishes,
Call'd him an evil of their own electing.
And is their ignorant zeal so fiery now
When all their thanks are cold? The mutable hearts
That move in their false breasts! Provide me safety!

[Shout.

Hark, I hear ruin threaten me with a voice
That imitates thunder.

[Enter **GENTLEMAN**.

GENTLEMAN
Where's the king?

VORTIGER
Who takes him?

GENTLEMAN
Send peace to all your royal thoughts, my lord;
A fleet of valiant Saxons newly landed
Offer the truth of all their service to you.

VORTIGER
Saxons! My wishes! Let 'em have free entrance
And plenteous welcomes from all hearts that love us;
They never could come happier.

[Enter **HENGIST**, **HORUS**, drum and **SOLDIERS**.

HENGIST
Health, power, and victory to Vortiger.

VORTIGER
There can be no more wish'd to a king's pleasure
If all the languages earth speaks were ransack'd.
Your names I know not, but so much good fortune
And warranted worth lightens your fair aspects,
I cannot but in arms of love enfold you.

HENGIST
The mistress of our births, hope-fruitful Germany,
Calls me Hengistus, and this Captain Horsus,
A man low built but, sir, in acts of valour
Flame is not swifter. We are all, my lord,
The sons of fortune; she has sent us forth
To thrive by the red sweat of our own merits,
And since after the rage of many a tempest
Our fate has cast us upon Britain's bounds,
We offer you the first fruits of our wounds.

VORTIGER
Which we shall dearly prize; the mean'st blood spent
Shall at wealth's fountain make his own content.

HENGIST
You double vigour in us then, my lord:
Pay is the soul of them that thrive by th' sword.

[Exeunt **OMNES**.

Alarums and skirmish. Enter **VORTIGER** and **GENTLEMAN**.

GENTLEMAN
My lord, these Saxons bring a fortune with 'em
Stains any Roman success.

VORTIGER
On, speak forward;
I will not take a moment from thy tidings.

GENTLEMAN
The main supporters of this insurrection
They have taken prisoners, and the rest so tame
They stoop to the least grace that flows from mercy.

VORTIGER
Never came power guided by better stars
Than these men's fortitudes, yet th'are misbelievers;
'Tis to my reason wondrous.

[Enter **HENGIST, HORUS**, with drum, colours, **SOLDIERS** leading **PRISONERS**.

Y'have given me such a first taste of your worth,
'Twill never from my love; sure when life's gone
The memory sure will follow, my soul still
Participating immortality with it.
And here's the misery of earth's limited glory:
There's not a way reveal'd to give you honour
Above the sum which your own praises give you.

HENGIST
Indeed, my lord, we hold, when all's summ'd up
That can be made for worth to be express'd,
The fame that a man wins himself is best;
That he may call his own: honours put to him
Make him no more a man than his clothes do,
And as soon taken off, for as in warmth
The heat comes from the body, not the weeds,
So man's true fame must strike from his own deeds.
And since by this event which fortune speaks us
This land appears the fair predestin'd soil
Ordain'd for our good hap, we crave, my lord,
A little earth to thrive on, what you please,
Where we'll but keep a nursery of good spirits
To fight for you and yours.

VORTIGER
Sir, for our treasure,
'Tis open to your merits as our love,
But for y'are strangers in religion chiefly,
Which is the greatest alienation can be
And breeds most factions in the bloods of men,
I must not grant you that.

[Enter **SIMON** with a hide.

HENGIST [Aside]
'S precious!—My lord,
I see a pattern, be it but so little
As yon poor hide will compass.

VORTIGER
How! The hide?

HENGIST
Rather than nothing, sir.

VORTIGER
Since y'are so reasonable,
Take so much in the best part of our kingdom.

HENGIST
We thank your grace.

[Exit **VORTIGER**.]

Rivers from bubbling springs
Have rise at first, and great from abject things.
Stay yonder fellow. He came luckily,
And he shall fare well for't, whate'er he be;
We'll thank our fortune in rewarding him.

HORSUS
Stay, fellow.

SIMON
How, fellow! 'Tis more than you know
Whether I be your fellow or no, for I am sure
You see me not.

HENGIST
Come, what's the price of your hide?

SIMON [Aside]

Oh, unreasonable villain! He would buy the house o'er a man's head. I'll be sure now to make my bargain wisely; they may buy me out of my skin else.—Whose hide would you have, mine or the beast's? There's little difference in their complexions; I think mine be th' better o' th' twain: you shall see for your love and buy for your money. [Aside] A pestilence on you all, how have you gull'd me! You buy an ox hide! You buy a good calf's gather! They are all hungry soldiers and I took 'em for shoemakers.

HENGIST

Hold fellow, prithee hold. Right a fool wordling
That kicks at all good fortune! Whose man art thou?

SIMON

I am a servant, yet I am a masterless man, sir.

HENGIST

How! Prithee how's that now?

SIMON

Very nimbly, sir: my master's dead, and I serve my mistress. I am a masterless man, sir; she's now a widow, and I am the foreman of her tan-pit.

HENGIST [Giving him money]

Hold you and thank your fortune, not your wit.

SIMON

Faith, and I thank your bounty and not your wisdom; you are not troubled greatly with wit neither it seems. [Aside] Now by this light, a nest of yellowhammers! What will become of me? If I can keep all these without hanging of myself, I am happier than a hundred of my neighbours.—You shall have my skin into the bargain too, willingly, sir, then if I chance to die like a dog, the labour will be saved of fleaing. I'll undertake, sir, you shall have all the skins of our parish at this rate, man and woman's.

HENGIST

Sirrah, give ear to me: now take your hide
And cut it all into the slenderest thongs
That can bear strength to hold.

SIMON

That were a jest indeed! Go and spoil all the leather? Sin and pity, why, 'twould shoe half your army!

HENGIST

Do't, I bid you.

SIMON

What, cut it all in thongs? Hunch, this is like the vanity of your Roman gallants, that cannot wear good suits but they must have 'em cut and slash'd into giggets, that the very crimson taffety sits blushing at their follies. I would I might persuade you, sir, from the humour of cutting; 'tis but a kind of swaggering condition and nothing profitable. What an't were but well pinked? 'Twould last longer for a summer suit.

HENGIST
What a gross lump of ignorance have I lighted on!
I must be forc'd to beat my drift into him.
Look you, to make you wiser than your parents,
I have so much ground given me as this hide will compass,
Which, as it is, is nothing.

SIMON
Nothing, quoth 'a!
Why, 'twill not keep a hog!

HENGIST
Now with the vantage
Cut into several parcels, 'twill stretch far
And make a liberal circuit.

SIMON
A shame on your crafty hide! Is this your cunning? I have learn'd more knavery now than ever I shall
shake off while I live. I'll go purchase lands by cows' tails and undo the parish; three good bulls' pizzles
would set up a man forever. This is like a pin a day doubled to set up a haberdasher of small wares.

HENGIST
Thus men as mean to thrive as we must learn, captain,
Set in a foot at first.

SIMON
A foot do you call it?
The devil's in that foot, it takes up all
This leather.

HENGIST
Dispatch, away, and cut it carefully
With all the advantage, sirrah.

SIMON
You could never have lighted upon such a fellow, captain, to serve your turn. I have such a trick of
stretching too—I learnt it of a tanner's man that was hang'd last sessions—that I'll warrant you I'll get
you in a mile and a half more than y'are aware of.

HENGIST
Pray serve me so as oft as you will, sir.

SIMON
I'm casting about for nine acres to make you a garden plot out of one of the buttocks.

HENGIST
'Twill be a good soil for nosegays.

SIMON
'Twill be a good soil for cabbages to stuff out the guts of your fellows there.

[Exit **SIMON**.

HENGIST
You, sirs, go see it carefully perform'd;
It is the first foundations of our fortunes
On Britain's earth and ought to be embrac'd
With a respect near-link'd to adoration.

[Exeunt **SOLDIERS**.

Methinks it sounds to me a fair assurance
Of large honours and hopes, does't not, captain?

HORSUS
How many have begun with less at first
That have departed emperors from their bodies,
And left their carcasses as much in monument
As would erect a college?

HENGIST
There's the fruits
Of their religious shows too, to lie rotting
Under a million spent in gold and marble,
When thousands left behind dies without shelter,
Having nor house nor food.

HORSUS
A precious charity.
But where shall we make choice of our ground, captain?

HENGIST
About the fruitful banks of uberous Kent,
A fat and olive soil; there we came in.
Oh, captain, h'as given he knows not what!

HORSUS
Long may he give so.

HENGIST
I tell thee, sirrah, he that begg'd a field
Of fourscore acres for a garden plot,
'Twas pretty well, but he came short of this.

HORSUS
Send over for more Saxons.

HENGIST
With all speed, captain.

HORSUS
Especially for Roxena.

HENGIST
Who, my daughter?

HORSUS
That star of Germany, forget not her, sir,
She is a fair, fortunate maid—aside I shall betray myself—
Fair is she, and most fortunate may she be.
[Aside] But in maid lost forever: my desire
Has been the close confusion of that name.
A treasure 'tis, able to make more thieves
Than cabinets set open to entice,
Which learns one theft that never knew the vice.

HENGIST
Some I'll dispatch with speed.

HORSUS
Do you forget not.

HENGIST
Marry, pray help my memory if I should.

HORSUS
Roxena, you remember?

HENGIST
What more dear, sir?

HORSUS
I see you need no help; your memory's clear, sir.

[Shout and flourish.

HENGIST
Those shouts leapt from our army.

HORSUS
They were too cheerful
To voice a bad event.

[Enter **GENTLEMAN SAXON**.

HENGIST
Now, sir, your news?

GENTLEMAN SAXON
Roxena the fair.

HENGIST
True, she shall be sent for.

GENTLEMAN SAXON
She's here.

HENGIST
What sayst?

GENTLEMAN SAXON
She's come, sir.

HORSUS [Aside]
A new youth
Begins me o'er again!

GENTLEMAN SAXON
Followed you close, sir,
With such a zeal as daughter never equall'd,
Expos'd herself to all the merciless dangers
Set in mankind or fortune, not regarding
Aught but your sight.

HENGIST
Her love is infinite to me.

HORSUS [Aside]
Most charitably censor'd! 'Tis her cunning,
The love of her own lust, which makes a woman
Gallop down hill as fearless as a drunkard;
There's no true lodestone i' th' world but that.
It draws 'em through all storms by sea or shame:
Life's loss is thought too small to pay that game.

GENTLEMAN SAXON
What follows more of her will take you strongly.

HENGIST
How!

GENTLEMAN SAXON

Nay, 'tis worth your wonder.

HENGIST
I thirst for't.

GENTLEMAN SAXON
Her heart joy-ravish'd at your late success,
Being the early morning of your fortunes
So prosperously new-opening at her coming,
She takes a cup of gold and midst the army,
Teaching her knee a current cheerfulness
Which well became her, drank a liberal health
To the king's joys and yours, the king in presence,
Who with her sight, but her behaviour chiefly—
Or chief I know not which, but one or both—
But he's so far 'bove my expression caught,
'Twere art enough for [one] man's time and portion
To speak him and miss nothing.

HENGIST
This is astonishing!

HORSUS [Aside]
Oh, this ends bitter now! Our close hid flame
Will break out of my heart: I cannot keep it.

HENGIST
Gave you attention to this, captain? How now, man?

HORSUS
A kind of grief about these times o' th' moon still;
I feel a pain like a convulsion,
A cramp at heart, I know not what name fits it.

HENGIST
Nor never seek one for't; let it go
Without a name. Would all griefs were serv'd so;
Our using of 'em mannerly makes 'em grow.

[Flourish. Enter **VORTIGER, ROXENA, ATTENDANTS.**

HORSUS [Aside]
A love knot already, arm in arm!

VORTIGER
What's he lays claim here?

HENGIST

In right of fatherhood
I challenge an obedient part, my lord.

VORTIGER
Take 't, and send back the rest.

HENGIST
What means your grace?

VORTIGER
You'll keep no more than what belongs to you, will you?

HENGIST
That's all, my lord, it all belongs to me; yet
I keep a husband's interest till he come.
Yet out of duty and respect of majesty,
I send her back your servant.

VORTIGER
My mistress, sir, or nothing.

HENGIST
Come again;
I never thought to have heard so ill of thee.

VORTIGER
How, sir! So ill?

HENGIST
So beyond detestable,
To be an honest vassal is some calling;
Poor is the worst of that, shame comes not to't.
But mistress: that's the only common bait
Fortune sets at all hours, catching whores with it,
And plucks 'em up by clusters. There's my sword, my lord,
And if your strong desires aim at my blood,
Which runs too purely there, a nobler way
Quench it in mine.

VORTIGER
I ne'er took sword in vain.
Hengist, we here create thee Earl of Kent.

HORSUS [Aside, and falling down]
Oh, that will do't, 'twill do't!

VORTIGER
What ails our friend? Look to him.

ROXENA

Oh, 'tis his epilepsy, I know it well;
I holp him once in Germany. Com'st again?
A virgin's right hand strok'd upon his heart
Gives him ease straight, but 't must be a pure virgin,
Or else it brings no comfort.

VORTIGER [Aside]

What a task
She puts upon herself! Unurg'd-for purity!
The proof of this will bring love's rage upon me.

[**ROXENA** kneels by **HORSUS**, and they talk aside.

ROXENA

Oh, this would mad a woman! There's no plague
In love to indiscretion.

HORSUS

Pish, this cures not.

ROXENA

Dost think I'll ever wrong thee?

HORSUS

Oh, most feelingly!
But I'll prevent it now and break thy neck
With thy own cunning; thou hast undertook
To give me help, to bring in royal credit,
Thy crack'd virginity, but I'll spoil all:
I will not stand on purpose, though I could,
But fall still, to disgrace thee.

ROXENA

What, you will not?

HORSUS

I have no other way to help myself,
For when thou't known to be a whore impost'rous,
I shall be sure to keep thee.

ROXENA

Oh, sir, shame me not!
Y'have had what's precious; try my faith yet once more:
Undo me not at first in chaste opinion.

HORSUS

All this art shall not make me find my legs.

ROXENA
I prithee wilt thou wilfully confound me?

HORSUS
Well, I'm content for this time to recover
To save thy credit and bite in my pain,
But if thou ever fail'st me, I will fall
And thou shalt never get me up again.

ROXENA
Agreed 'twixt you and I, sir.—

[Raising him.

See, my lord,
A poor maid's work: the man may pass for health now
Among the clearest bloods and whose are nicest.

VORTIGER
I have heard of women bring men on their knees,
But few that e'er restor'd 'em. How now, captain?

HORSUS
My lord, methinks I could do things past man,
I'm so renew'd in vigour; I long most
For violent exercise to take me down:
My joy's so high in blood I am above frailty.

VORTIGER
My Lord of Kent?

HENGIST
Your love's unworthy creature.

VORTIGER
Seest thou this fair chain? Think upon the means
To keep it link'd forever.

HENGIST
Oh, my lord,
'Tis many degrees sund'red from that hope!
Besides your grace has a young, virtuous queen.

VORTIGER
I say think on't, think on't.

HORSUS [Aside]
And this wind hold
I shall even fall to my old disease again.

VORTIGER [To **ROXENA**]
There's no fault in thee but to come so late;
All else is excellent, I chide none but fate.

[Flourish, cornets. Exeunt.

SCENE I - A Room in the Palace

Enter **HORSUS, ROXENA**.

ROXENA
I have no conceit now that you ever lov'd me,
But as lust held you for the time.

HORSUS
So, so.

ROXENA
Do you pine at my advancement, sir?

HORSUS
Oh, barrenness
Of understanding! What a right love is this!
'Tis you that fall, I that am reprehended!
What height of honours, eminence and fortune
Should ravish me from you?

ROXENA
Who can tell that, sir? What's he can judge
Of a man's appetite before he sees him eat?
Who knows the strength of any's constancy
That never yet was tempted? We can call
Nothing our own if they be deeds to come;
They are only ours when they are pass'd and done.
How bless'd are you above your apprehension
If your desire would lend you so much patience
To examine the adventurous condition
Of our affections, which are full of hazard,
And draw in the time's goodness to defend us!
First, this bold course of ours can't last long,

Or never does in any without shame,
And that, you know, brings danger; and the greater
My father is in blood, as he's well risen,
The greater will the storm of his rage be
'Gainst his blood's wronging; I have cast for this.
'Tis not advancement that I love alone,
'Tis love of shelter, to keep shame unknown.

HORSUS
Oh, were I sure of thee, as 'tis impossible
There to be ever sure where there's no hold,
Your pregnant hopes should not be long arising!

ROXENA
By what assurance have you held me thus far
Which you found firm, despair you not in that.

HORSUS
True, that was good security for the time,
But admit a change of state. When y'are advanc'd
You women have a French toy in your pride;
You make your friend come crouching, or perhaps,
To bow i' th' hams the better, he is put
To complement three hours with your chief gentlewoman,
Then perhaps not admitted, nay, nor never:
That's the more noble fashion. Forgetfulness:
'Tis the pleasing'st virtue anyone can have
That rises up from nothing, for by the same
Forgetting all they forget from whence they came,
An excellent property for oblivion.

ROXENA
I pity all the fortunes of poor women
Now in mine own unhappiness. When we have given
All that we have to men, what's our requital?
An ill-fac'd jealousy, which resembles much
The mistrustfulness of an insatiate thief
That scarce believes he has all, though he has stripp'd
The true man naked and left nothing on him
But the hard cord that binds him: so are we
First robb'd and then left bound by jealousy.
Sure he that finds us now has a great purchase,
And well he gains that builds another's ruins,
Yet man—the only seed that's sown in envy,
Whom little would suffice as any creature
Either in food or pleasure—yet 'tis known
What would give ten enough contents not one.
A strong diseas'd conceit may tell strange tales to you

And so abuse us both: take but th' opinion
Of common reason, and you'll find 't impossible
That you should lose me in this king's advancement,
Who here's a usurper. As he has the kingdom,
So shall he have my love by usurpation;
The right shall be in thee still: my ascension
To dignity is but to waft thee upward,
And all usurpers have a falling-sickness,
They cannot keep up long.

HORSUS
May credulous man
Put all his confidence in so weak a bottom
And make a saving voyage?

ROXENA
Nay, as gainful
As ever man yet made.

HORSUS
Go, take thy fortune,
Aspire with my consent, so thy ambition
Will be sure to prosper. Speak the fair certainty
Of Britain's queen home to thy wishes.

ROXENA
Speak
In hope I may, but not in certainty.

HORSUS
I say in both: hope and be sure I'll quickly
Remove her that stands between thee and thy glory.

ROXENA
Life is love!
If lost virginity can win such a day,
I'll have no daughter but shall learn my way.

[Exit **ROXENA**.

HORSUS
'Twill be good work for him that first instructs 'em,
Maybe some son of mine, got by this woman too.
Man's scattered lust brings forth most strange events,
An' 'twere but strictly thought on. How many brothers
Wantonly got through ignorance of their births
May match with their own sisters!

[Enter **VORTIGER**.

[Aside] Peace, 'tis he.
Invention fail me not; 'tis a gallant's credit
To marry his whore bravely.

VORTIGER [Aside]
Have I power
Of life and death, and cannot command ease
In mine own blood? After I was a king
I thought I never should have felt pain more,
That there had been a ceasing of all passions
And common stings, which subjects use to feel,
That were created with a patience fit
For all extremities: but such as we
Know not the way to suffer; then to do't,
How most prepost'rous 'tis! What's all our greatness
If we that prescribe bounds to meaner men
Must not pass these ourselves? Oh, most ridiculous!
This makes the vulgar merry to endure,
Knowing our state is strict and less secure.
I'll break through custom. Why should not the mind,
The nobler part that's of us, be allow'd
Change of affections, as our bodies are
Still change of food and raiment? I'll have't so.
All fashions appear strange at first production,
But this would be well followed.—Oh, captain!

HORSUS
My lord, I grieve for you; you scarce fetch breath
But a sigh hangs at end on't: this is no way
If you'll give way to counsel.

VORTIGER
Set me right then,
And quickly, sir, or I shall curse thy charity
For lifting up my understanding to me
To show that I was wrong: ignorance is safe;
I slept happily. If knowledge mend me not
Thou hast committed a most cruel sin,
To wake me into judgment and then leave me.

HORSUS
I will not leave you so, sir, that were rudely done.
First y'have a flame too open and too violent,
Which like blood-guiltiness in an offender
Betrays him when none can: out with it, sir,
Or let some cunning coverture be made

Before our practice enters, 'twill spoil all else.

VORTIGER
Why, look you, sir, I can be as calm as silence
All the whiles music plays; strike on, sweet friend,
As mild and merry as the heart of innocence.
I prithee take my temper. Has a virgin
A heat more modest?

HORSUS [Aside]
He does well to ask me;
I could have told that once.—Why, here's a government!
There's not a sweeter amity in friendship
Than in this friendly league 'twixt you and health.

VORTIGER
Then since thou find'st me capable of happiness,
Instruct me with the practice.

HORSUS
What would you say, my lord,
If I ensnare her in an act of lust?

VORTIGER
Oh, there were art to the life! But that's impossible;
I prithee flatter me no further with't.
Fie, so much sin as goes to make up that
Will ne'er prevail with her: why, I tell thee, sir,
She's so sin-killing modest, that if only
To move the question were enough adultery
To cause a separation, there's no gallant
So brassy-impudent durst undertake
The words that should belong to't.

HORSUS
Say you so, sir?
There's nothing made i' th' world but has a way to't,
Though some be harder than the rest to find,
Yet one there is, that's certain, and I think
I have took the course to light on't.

VORTIGER
Oh, I pray for't!

HORSUS
I heard you lately say, from whence, my lord,
My practice receiv'd life first, that your queen
Still consecrates her time to contemplation,

Takes solitary walks.

VORTIGER
Nay, late and early, sir,
Commands her weak guard from her, which are but women
When 'tis at strongest.

HORSUS
I like all this well, my lord.
And now your grace shall know what net is us'd
In many places to catch modest women,
Such as will never yield by prayers or gifts.
Now there be some will catch up men as fast,
But those she-fowlers nothing concerns us:
Their birding is at windows, ours abroad,
Where ring-doves should be caught, that's married wives
Or chaste maids, what the appetite has a mind to.
'Tis practis'd often, therefore worth discovery
And may well fit the purpose.

VORTIGER
Make no pause then.

HORSUS
The honest gentlewoman, where'er she be,
When nothing will prevail, I pity her now;
Poor soul, she's entic'd forth by her own sex
To be betray'd to man, who in some garden-house
Or remote walk, taking his lustful time,
Binds darkness on her eyes, surprises her,
And having a coach ready, turns her in,
Hurrying her where he list for the sin's safety,
Making a rape of honour without words,
And at the low ebbs of his lust, perhaps
Some three days after, sends her coach again
To the same place, and, which would make most mad,
She's spoil'd of all, yet knows not where she was robb'd:
Wise, dear, precious mischief.

VORTIGER
Is this practis'd?

HORSUS
Too much, my lord, to be so little known;
A springe to catch a maidenhead after sunset,
Clip it, and send it home again to th' city:
There 'twill be ne'er perceiv'd.

VORTIGER
My raptures want expression! I conceit
Enough to make me fortunate and thee great.

HORSUS
Ay, practise it then, my lord. [Aside] I knew 'twould take.

[Exeunt.

SCENE II - Grounds Near the Palace

Enter **CASTIZA** with a book, two **LADIES**.

CASTIZA
Methinks you live strange lives! When I see't not,
The less it grieves me; you know how to ease me then.
If you but knew how well I lov'd your absence
You would bestow 't upon me without asking.

FIRST LADY
Faith, for my part, were it no more for ceremony
Than 'tis for love, you should walk long enough
For my attendance; so think all my fellows,
Though they say nothing. Books in women's hands
They are as much against the hair, methinks,
As to see men wear stomachers and night-rails!
She that has the green sickness and should follow her counsel would die like an ass and go to th' worms like a salad; not I as long as such a creature as man is made: she's a fool that will not know what he's good for.

[Exeunt **LADIES**.

CASTIZA
Though amongst lives' elections that of virgin
I speak noblest of, yet 't has pleas'd just heaven
To send me a contented blessedness
In this of marriage, which I ever doubted;
I see the king's affection was a true one,
It lasts and holds out long: that['s] no mean virtue
In a commanding man, though in great fear
At first I was enforc'd to venture on't.

[Enter **VORTIGER** and **HORSUS** disguised, to one side.

VORTIGER
All's happy, clear and safe.

HORSUS
The rest comes gently then.

VORTIGER
Be sure you seize on her full sight at first,
For fear of my discovery.

HORSUS
I'll not miss it.

VORTIGER
Now fortune, and I am sped.

[**HORSUS** seizes and blindfolds **CASTIZA**.

CASTIZA
Oh, help, treason, treason!

HORSUS
Sirrah, how stand you? Prevent noise and clamour,
Or death shall end thy service.

VORTIGER [Aside]
A sure cunning.

CASTIZA
Oh, rescue!

HORSUS
Dead her voice; away, make speed!

[**VORTIGER** gags her. Exeunt and enter again.

SCENE III - Off a Country Road

CASTIZA
No help, no succour?

HORSUS
Louder yet?
Your voice to the last rack, you shall have leave now;
Y'are far from any pity.

CASTIZA
What's my sin?

HORSUS
Contempt of man, and he's a noble creature,
And takes it in ill part to be despis'd.

CASTIZA
I never despis'd any.

HORSUS
No? You hold us
Unworthy to be lov'd. What call you that?

CASTIZA
I have a lord disproves you.

HORSUS
Pish, your lord!
You're bound to love your lord, that's no thanks to you;
You should love those you are not tied to love:
That's the right trial of a woman's charity.

CASTIZA
I know not what you are nor what my fault is,
But if't be life you seek, whate'er you be,
Use no immodest words and take it from me:
You kill me more in talking sinfully
Than acting cruelly; be so far pitiful
To end me without words.

HORSUS
Long may you live,
The wish of a good subject; 'tis not life
That I thirst after: loyalty forbid
I should commit such treason! You mistake me,
I have no such bloody thought; only your love
Shall content me.

CASTIZA
What said you, sir?

HORSUS
Thus, thus plainly,
To strip my words as naked as my purpose,
I must and will enjoy you.

[**CASTIZA** swoons.

Gone already?

Look to her, bear her up, she goes apace.
I fear'd this still, and therefore came provided.

[Takes out a vial and gives some of its liquid to **CASTIZA**.

There's that will fetch life from a dying spark
And make it spread a furnace; she's well straight.
It kept a lord seven years alive together
In spite of nature, that he look'd like one
Had leave to walk out of a grave to air himself
Yet still walked lord.

[**CASTIZA** recovers.

Pish, let her go; she stands,
Upon my knowledge, or else she counterfeits.
I know the virtue.

CASTIZA
Never did sorrows in afflicted woman
Meet with such cruelty; such hard-hearted ways
Human invention never found before.
To call back life to live is but ill-taken
By some departing soul; then to force mine back
To an eternal act of death in lust,
What is it but most execrable?

HORSUS
So, so;
But this is from the business. List to me:
Here you are now far from all hope of friendship,
Save what you make mine; 'scape me you cannot,
Send your soul that assurance. That resolv'd on
You know not who I am nor never shall,
I need not fear you then; but give consent
Then with the faithfulness of a true friend:
I'll open myself to you, fall your servant,
As I do now in hope, proud of submission,
And seal the deed up with eternal secrecy,
Not death should pick it open, much less the king's
Authority or torture.

VORTIGER [Aside]
I admire him.

CASTIZA [Kneeling]
Oh, sir, whate'er you are, I teach my knee
Thus to requite you; be content to take

Only my sight as ransom for mine honour,
And where you have but mock'd mine eyes with darkness,
Pluck 'em out quite: all outward light of body
I'll spare most willingly, but take not from me
That which must guide me to another world
And leave me dark forever, fast without
That cursed pleasure which would make two souls
Endure a famine everlastingly.

HORSUS [Aside]
This almost moves.

VORTIGER [Aside]
By this light, he'll be taken.

HORSUS [Aside]
I'll wrastle down all pity.—Will you consent?

CASTIZA
I'll never be so guilty.

HORSUS
Farewell words then;
You hear no more of me, but thus I seize thee.

CASTIZA
Oh, if a power above be reverenc'd in thee,
I bind thee by that name, by manhood, nobleness,
And all the charms of honour!

[Exeunt **VORTIGER** carrying off **CASTIZA**.

HORSUS
Here's one caught
For an example; never was poor lady
So mock'd into false terror. With what anguish
She lies with her own lord! Now she could curse
All into barrenness and beguile herself by it.
Conceit's a powerful thing, and is indeed
Plac'd as a palate to taste grief or love,
And as that relishes so we approve:
Hence it comes that our taste is so beguil'd,
Changing pure blood for some that's mix'd and soil'd.

[Exit.

SCENE IV - A Chamber in a Castle Near Quinborough

Enter **HENGIST**.

HENGIST
A fair and fortunate constellation reign'd
When we set footing here: from his first gift,
Which to a king's unbounded eyes seem'd nothing,
The compass of a hide, I have erected
A strong and spacious castle, yet contain'd myself
Within my limits, without check or censure.
Thither, with all the observance of a subject,
The liveliest witness of a grateful mind,
I purpose to invite him and his queen
And feast 'em nobly.

[A noise. **BARBER** and **TAILOR** within.

BARBER [Within]
We will enter, sir;
'Tis a state business of a twelvemonth long,
The choosing of a mayor.

HENGIST
What noise is that?

TAILOR [Within]
Sir, we must speak with the good Earl of Kent;
Though we were ne'er brought up to keep a door,
We are as honest, sir, as some that do.

[Enter **GENTLEMAN SAXON**.

HENGIST
Now what's the occasion of their clamours, sir?

GENTLEMAN SAXON
Please you, my lord, a company of townsmen
Are bent against all denials and resistance
To have speech with your lordship, and that you
Must end a difference, which none else can do.

HENGIST
Why, then there's reason in their violence,
Which I never look'd for: let in first but one,
And as we relish him the rest comes on.

[Exit **GENTLEMAN SAXON**.

'Twere no safe wisdom in a rising man
To slight off such as these; nay, rather these
Are the foundation of a lofty work:
We cannot build without them and stand sure;
He that ascends up to a mountain's top
Must first begin at foot.

[Enter **GENTLEMAN SAXON**.

Now, sir, who comes?

GENTLEMAN SAXON
They cannot yet agree, my lord, of that.

HENGIST
How!

GENTLEMAN SAXON
They say 'tis worse now for 'em than ever 'twas before,
For where the difference stood but between two,
Upon this coming first they are at odds;
One says, sir, he shall lose his place at church by't,
Another he'll not do his wife that wrong,
And by their good wills they would come all at first.
The strife continues in most heat, my lord,
Between a country barber and a tailor
Of the same town, and which your lordship names
'Tis yielded by consent that one shall enter.

HENGIST
Here's no sweet coil! I'm glad they're so reasonable.
Call in the barber: if the tale be long
He'll cut it short, I trust; that's all the hope on't.

[Enter **BARBER**.

Now, sir, are you the barber?

BARBER
Oh, most barbarous! A corrector of enormities in hair, my lord, a promoter of upper lips, or what your
lordship, in the neatness of your discretion, shall vouchsafe call it.

HENGIST
Very good, I see this you have without book.
But what's your business now?

BARBER

Your lordship comes
To a high point indeed; the business, sir,
Lies all about the head.

HENGIST
That's work for you.

BARBER
No, my good lord, there is a corporation, a kind of body, a body.

HENGIST
The barber's out at body, let in the tailor.
This 'tis to reach beyond your own profession:
When you let go your head, you lose your memory;
You have no business with the body.

BARBER
Yes, sir, I am a barber-surgeon: I have had something to do with't in my time, my lord, and I was never so out o' th' body as I have been here of late; send me good luck, I'll go marry some whore or other but I'll get in again.

[Enter **TAILOR**.

HENGIST
Now, sir, a good discovery come from you
That we may know the inwards of the business.

TAILOR
I will rip up the linings to your lordship,
And show what stuff 'tis made on; for the body,
Or corporation—

HENGIST
There the barber left indeed.

TAILOR
'Tis piec'd up of two factions.

HENGIST
A patch'd town the whilst.

TAILOR
Nor can we go through stitch, my noble lord,
The choler is so great in the one party.
And as in linsey-woolsey wove together
One piece makes several suits, so, upright earl,
Our linsey-woolsey hearts makes all this coil.

HENGIST
What's all this now?
Call in the rest; I'm ne'er the wiser yet.
I should commend my wit could I but guess
What this would come to.

[Enter **GLOVER, BUTTONMONGER, BRAZIER** and the other **TRADESMEN**.

Now, sirs, what are you?

GLOVER
Sir-reverence on your lordship, I am a glover.

HENGIST
What needs that then?

GLOVER
Sometimes I deal with dog's-leather,
Sir-reverence all that while.

HENGIST
Well, to the purpose, if there be any towards.

GLOVER
I were an ass else, saving your lordship's presence; we have a body, but our town wants a hand, a hand of justice, a worshipful master mayor.

HENGIST
This is well-handed yet,
A man may take some hold on't. You want a mayor?

GLOVER
Right, but there's two at fisticuffs about it, sir,
As I may say, at daggers drawing, sir,
But that I cannot say, because they have none;
And you being Earl of Kent, the town does say
Your lordship's voice shall choose and part the fray.

HENGIST
This is strange work for me. Well, sir, what be they?

GLOVER
The one is a tanner.

HENGIST
Fie, I shall be too partial;
I owe too much affection to that trade
To put it to my voice. What is his name?

GLOVER
Simon, sir.

HENGIST
How! Simon, too?

GLOVER
Nay, 'tis but Simon one, sir, the very same Simon
That sold your lordship the hide.

HENGIST
What sayst thou?

GLOVER
That's all his glory, sir: he got his master's widow by't presently after, a rich tanner's wife. She has set
him up; he was her foreman a long time in her other husband's days.

HENGIST
Now let me perish in my first aspiring
If the pretty simplicity of his fortune
Do not most highly take me; 'tis a presage, methinks,
Of bright, succeeding happiness to mine
When my fate's glowworm casts forth such a shine.
And what's the other that contends with him?

TAILOR
Marry, my noble lord, a fustian weaver.

HENGIST
How! Will he offer to compare with Simon?
He a fit match for him!

[Enter **SIMON** and **OLIVER**.

BARBER
Hark, hark, my lord!
Here they come both now in a pelting chafe
From the town-house.

SIMON
How! Before me? I scorn thee,
Thou wattle-fac'd, sing'd pig!

OLIVER
Pig? I defy thee!
My uncle was a Jew and scorn'd the motion.

SIMON

I list not brook thy vaunts. Compare with me?
Thou spindle of concupiscence, 'tis well known
Thy first wife was a flax-wench.

OLIVER

But such a flax-wench
Would I might never want at my most need,
Nor any friend of mine. My neighbours knew her;
Thy wife was but a hampen halter to her.

SIMON

Use better words; I'll hang thee in my year else,
Let whose will choose thee afterwards.

GLOVER

Peace! For shame!
Quench your great spirits. Do not you see his lordship?

HENGIST

What, Master Simonides?

SIMON

Simonides? What a fine name he has made of Simon! Then he's an ass that calls me Simon again; I'm quite out of love with't.

HENGIST

Give me thy hand. I love thee and thy fortunes;
I like a man that thrives.

SIMON

I took a widow, my lord, to be the best piece of ground to thrive on, and by my faith, there's a young Simonides, like a green onion, peeping up already.

HENGIST

Th'ast a good, lucky hand.

SIMON

I have somewhat, sir.

HENGIST

But why to me is this election offer'd?
The choosing of a mayor goes by most voices.

SIMON

True, sir, but most of our townsmen are so hoarse with drinking, there's ne'er a good voice amongst 'em all that are now here in this company.

HENGIST
Are you content both to put all to these then,
To whom I liberally resign my interest
To prevent censure?

SIMON
I speak first, my lord.

OLIVER
Though I speak last, I hope I am not least.
If they will cast away a town-born child,
They may; 'tis but dying some forty years or so
Before my time.

HENGIST
I'll leave you to your choice awhile.

ALL
Your good lordship.

[Exit **HENGIST**.

SIMON
Look you, neighbours, view us both well ere you be too hasty; let Oliver the fustian weaver stand as fair as I do, and the devil give him good out.

OLIVER
I do, thou upstart callymoocher, I do. 'Tis well known to thee I have been twice alecunner, thou mushrump that shot up in one night with lying with thy mistress.

SIMON
Faith, thou art such a spiny bald-rib, all the mistresses in the town would never get thee up.

OLIVER
I scorn to rise by a woman, as thou didst; my wife shall rise by me.

SIMON
The better for some of thy neighbours when you are asleep.

GLOVER
I pray cease of your communication; we can do nothing else.

[The **TRADESMEN** retire and talk amongst themselves.

OLIVER [Aside]
I gave that barber a fustian suit, and twice redeem'd his cittern; he may remember me.

SIMON [Aside]

I fear no false measure but in that tailor;
The glover and the button-maker are both cocksure;
That collier's eye I like not.
Now they consult, the matter is a-brewing.
Poor Gill my wife lies longing for this news;
'Twill make her a glad mother.

ALL
A Simon, a Simon, a Simon, a Simon!

SIMON
My good people, I thank you all.

OLIVER
Wretch that I am, tanner, thou hast curry'd favour.

SIMON
I curry? I defy thy fustian fume!

OLIVER
But I will prove a rebel all thy year
And raise up the seven deadly sins against thee.

[Exit.

SIMON
The deadly sins will scorn to rise by thee, and they have any breeding, as commonly they are well brought up; 'tis not for every scab to be acquainted with 'em. But leaving scabs, to you good neighbours now I bend my speech. First, to say more than a man can say, I hold it not so fit to be spoken, but to say what man ought to say, there I leave you also. I must confess your loves have chosen a weak and unlearn'd man—that I can neither write nor read you all can witness—yet not altogether so unlearn'd but I could set my mark to a bond, if I would be so simple, an excellent token of government. Cheer you then, my hearts, you have done you know not what. There's a full point; you must all cough and hem now.

ALL
Hum, hum, hum, cough!

SIMON
Now touching our common adversary, the fustian weaver, who threateneth he will raise the deadly sins amongst us, which as I take it are seven in number, let 'em come: our town's big enough to hold 'em, we will not much disgrace it; besides, you know a deadly sin will lie in a narrow hole. But when they think themselves safest and the web of their iniquity woven, with the horse-strength of my justice I'll break the looms of their concupiscence, and let the weaver go seek his shuttle. Here you may hem again, if you'll do me the favour.

ALL
Cough and hem!

SIMON

Why, I thank you all, and it shall not go unrewarded. Now for the seven deadly sins: first, for pride, which always sits uppermost and will be plac'd without a churchwarden; being a sin that is not like to be chargeable to the parish, I slip it over and think it not worthy of punishment. Now you all know that sloth does not anything; this place, you see, requires wisdom. How can a man in conscience punish that which does nothing? Envy, a poor, lean creature that eats raw liver, perhaps it pines to see me chosen, and that makes me the fatter with laughing; if I punish envy then I punish mine own carcass, a great sin against authority. For wrath, the less we say, the better 'tis; a scurvy, desperate thing it is, that commonly hangs itself and saves justice many a halter by't. Now for covetousness and gluttony, I'll tell you more when I come out of mine office; I shall have time to try what they are, I'll prove 'em soundly, and if I find gluttony and covetousness to be directly sins, I'll bury one i' th' bottom of a chest, and th'other i' th' end of my garden. But, sirs, for lechery, I mean to tickle that home, nay, I'm resolv'd upon't: I will not leave one whore in all the town.

BARBER

Some of your neighbours may go seek their wives i' th' country then.

SIMON

Barber, be silent; I will cut thy comb else. To conclude, I will learn the villainies of all trades, mine own I know already: if there be any knavery in the baker, I will bolt it out; if in the brewer, I will taste him throughly, and then piss out his iniquity in his own sinkhole. In a word, I will knock out all enormities like a bullock, and send the hide to my fellow tanners.

ALL

A Simonides, a true Simonides indeed!

[Enter **HENGIST** and **ROXENA**.

HENGIST

How now, how goes your choice?

TAILOR

Here's he, my lord.

SIMON

You may prove I am the man: I am bold to take the upper hand of your lordship a little; I'll not lose an inch of my honour.

HENGIST

Hold, sirs, there's some few crowns to mend your feast,
Because I like your choice.

[Gives them money.]

BARBER

Joy bless your lordship!
We'll drink your health with trumpets.

SIMON
Ay, with sackbutts,
That's the more solemn drinking for my state;
No malt this year shall fume into my pate.

[Exeunt all but **HENGIST** and **ROXENA**.

HENGIST
Continues still that fervour in his love?

ROXENA
Nay, with increase, my lord, the flames grows greater,
Though [he] has learn'd a better art of late
To set a screen before it.

[Enter **VORTIGER** and **HORSUS**.

HENGIST
Canst speak low?

[**HENGIST** and **ROXENA** retire to one side, **HENGIST** pretending to have fallen asleep reading a book.

HORSUS
Heard every word, my lord.

VORTIGER
Plainly?

HORSUS
Distinctly;
The course I took was dangerous, but not failing,
For I convey'd myself behind the hangings
Even first before her entrance.

VORTIGER
'Twas well ventur'd.

HORSUS
I had such a woman's first and second longing in me
To hear her how she would bear her mock'd abuse
After she was half return'd to privacy,
I could have fasted out an ember week,
And never thought of hunger, to have heard her;
She fetch'd three short turns, I shall ne'er forget 'em,
Like an imprison'd lark that offers still
Her wing at liberty and returns check'd:
So would her soul fain have been gone, and even hung

Flittering upon the bars of poor mortality,
Which ever as it offer'd, drove her back again.
Then came your holy Lupus and Germanus.

VORTIGER
Oh, two holy confessors.

HORSUS
At whose sight
I could perceive her fall upon her breast
And cruelly afflict herself with sorrow;
I never heard a sigh till I heard hers,
Who after her confession, pitying her,
Put her into a way of patience,
Which now she holds, to keep it hid from you.
There's all the pleasure that I took in't now,
When I heard that my pains was well rememb'red.
So with applying comforts and relief,
They have brought it low now to an easy grief,
But yet the taste is not quite gone.

VORTIGER
Still fortune
Sits bettering our invention.

[Enter **CASTIZA**.

HORSUS
Here she comes.

CASTIZA [Aside]
Yonder's my lord. Oh, I'll return again;
Methinks I should not dare to look on him.

HORSUS
She's gone again.

VORTIGER
It works the kindlier, sir;
Go now and call her back. She winds herself
Into the snare so prettily, 'tis a pleasure
To set toils for her.

[**HORSUS** brings **CASTIZA** back to **VORTIGER**.

CASTIZA [Aside]
He may read my shame
Now in my blush.

VORTIGER
Come, y'are so link'd to holiness,
So taken up with contemplative desires,
That the world has you yet enjoys you not;
You have been weeping too.

CASTIZA
Not I, my lord.

VORTIGER
Trust me, I fear you have; y'are much to blame
And you should yield so to passion without cause.
Is not there time enough for meditation?
Must it lay title to your health and beauty,
And draw them into time's consumption too?
'Tis too exacting for a holy faculty.
[Noticing **HENGIST**] My Lord of Kent? I pray wake him, captain;
He reads himself asleep sure.

HORSUS
My lord?

HENGIST
Your pardon, sir.

VORTIGER
Nay, I'll take away your book and bestow 't here.
Lady, you that delight in virgins' stories
And all chaste works, here's excellent reading for you;
Make of that book as rais'd men make of favour,
Which they grow sick to part from. And now, my lord,
You that have so conceitedly gone beyond me
And made such large use of a slender gift,
Which we never minded: I commend your thrift,
And for your building's name shall to all ages
Carry the stamp and impress of your wit,
It shall be call'd Thong Castle.

HENGIST
How, my lord!
Thong Castle! There your highness quits me kindly.

VORTIGER
'Tis fit art should be known by her right name;
You that can spread my gift, I'll spread your fame.

HENGIST

I thank your grace for that, sir.

VORTIGER
And, lov'd lord,
So well we do accept your invitation,
With all speed we'll set forward.

HENGIST
Your love honours me.

[Music. Exeunt **OMNES**.

ACT IV

SCENE I - A Road Near Thong Castle

Enter **VORTIGER, CASTIZA**, two **LADIES, ROXENA, DEVONSHIRE, STAFFORD** at one door, **SIMON** and his **BRETHREN** at the other, a mace and a sword before him.

SIMON
Lo, I the mayor of Quinborough town by name,
With all my brethren, saving one that's lame,
Are come as fast as fiery mill-horse gallops
To meet thy grace, thy queen and thy fair trollops.
For reason of our coming do not look,
It must be done, I found it i' th' town book;
And yet not I myself: I scorn to read,
I keep a clerk to do those jobs for need.
And now expect a rare conceit before Thong Castle see thee.
Reach me the thing to give the king, the other too I prithee.
Now here they be for queen and thee, the gifts all steel and leather,
But the conceit of mickle weight, and here they're come together:
To show two loves must join in one, our town presents to thee
This gilded scabbard to the queen, this dagger unto thee.

VORTIGER
Forbear your tedious and ridiculous duties!
I hate 'em, as I do the rotten roots of you,
You inconstant rabble; I have felt your fits.
Sheath up your bounty with your iron wits
And get you gone.

[Music. Exeunt **KING VORTIGER, CASTIZA, LORDS** and **LADIES**. Manent **SIMON** and **CITIZENS**.

SIMON
Look, sirs, is his back turn'd?

ALL
'Tis, 'tis.

SIMON
Then bless the good Earl of Kent, say I;
I'll have this dagger turn'd into a pie
And eaten up for anger, every bit on't.
And when that pie is new cut up by some rare, cunning pie-man,
They shall all lamentably sing, "Put up thy dagger, Simon."

[Exeunt.

SCENE II - A Hall in Thong Castle

Hoboys. The **KING VORTIGER** and his train met by **HENGIST** and **HORSUS**; they salute and exeunt. While the banquet is brought forth, music plays. Enter **VORTIGER, HENGIST, HORSUS, DEVONSHIRE, STAFFORD, CASTIZA, ROXENA**, and two **LADIES**.

HENGIST
A welcome, mighty lord, may appear costlier,
More full of talk and toil, show and conceit,
But one more stor'd with thankful love and truth
I forbid all the sons of men to boast of.

VORTIGER
Why, here's a fabric that implies eternity,
The building plain, but most substantial;
Methinks it looks as if it mock'd all ruin,
Save that great masterpiece of consumation,
The end of time, which must consume even ruin
And eat that into cinders.

HENGIST
There's no brass
Would last your praise, my lord; 'twould last beyond it
And shame our durablest metal.

VORTIGER [Taking him aside]
Horsus.

HORSUS
My lord.

VORTIGER
This is the time I have chosen; here's a full meeting,

And here will I disgrace her.

HORSUS
'Twill be sharp, my lord.

VORTIGER
Oh, 'twill be best, sir.

HORSUS
Why, here's the earl her father.

VORTIGER
Ay, and the lord her uncle, that's the height on't,
Invited both a' purpose to rise sick
Full of shame's surfeit.

HORSUS
And that's shrewd, byrlady;
It ever sticks close to the ribs of honour.
Great men are never sound men after it;
It leaves some ache or other in their names still,
Which their posterity feels at every weather.

VORTIGER
Mark but the least presentment of occasion;
As such times yields enough, and then mark me.

HORSUS
My observance is all yours, you know't, my lord.
[Aside] What careful ways some take t'abuse themselves!
But as there be assurers of men's goods
'Gainst storm or pirate, which gives venturers courage,
So such there must be to make up man's theft,
Or there would be no woman venturer left.
See, now they find their seats. What a false knot
Of amity he ties about her arm,
Which rage must part! In marriage 'tis no wonder
Knots knit with kisses are oft broke with thunder.

[Music.

Music? Then I have done, I always learn
To give my betters place.

VORTIGER
Where's Captain Horsus?

HORSUS

My lord.

VORTIGER
Sit, sit, we'll have a health anon
To all good services.

HORSUS
Th'are poor in these days;
They had rather have the cup than the health, my lord.
[Aside] I sit wrong now; he hears me not, and most
Great men are deaf on that side.

Song.
If in music were a power
To breath a welcome to thy worth,
This should be the ravishing hour
To vent her spirit's treasure forth.
Welcome, oh, welcome; in that word alone
She'ld choose to dwell and draw all parts to one.

VORTIGER
My Lord of Kent, I thank you for this welcome;
It came unthought of in the sweetest language
That ever my soul relish'd.

HENGIST
You are pleas'd, my lord,
To raise my happiness from slight deservings,
To show what power's in princes; not in us
Aught worthy, 'tis in you that makes us thus.
I'm chiefly sad, my lord, your queen's not merry.

VORTIGER [Aside]
So honour bless me, he has found the way
To my grief strangely.—Is there no delight?

CASTIZA
My lord, I wish not any, nor is't needful;
I am as I was ever.

VORTIGER
That's not so.

CASTIZA [Aside]
How? Oh, my fears!

VORTIGER
When she writ maid, my lord,

You knew her otherwise.

DEVONSHIRE
To speak but truth,
I never knew her a great friend to mirth,
Nor taken much with any one delight,
Though there be many seemly and honourable
To give content to ladies without taxing.

VORTIGER
My Lord of Kent, this to thy full desert,
Which intimates thy higher flow to honour.

[Drinks.]

HENGIST
Which, like a river, shall return service
To the great master-fountain.

VORTIGER [To **FIRST LADY**]
Where's your lord?
I miss'd him not till now. Lady, and yours?
No marvel then we were so out o' th' way
Of all pleasant discourse: they are the keys
Of human music; sure at their nativities
Great nature sign'd a general patent to 'em
To take up all the mirth in a whole kingdom.
What's their employment now?

FIRST LADY
May't please your grace,
We never are so far acquainted with 'em,
Nothing we know but what they cannot keep;
That's even the fashion of 'em all, my lord.

VORTIGER
It seems you have great faith though in their constancy,
And they in yours, you dare so trust each other.

SECOND LADY
Hope well we do, my lord; we have reason for't,
Because they say brown men are honestest,
But she's a fool will swear for any colour.

VORTIGER
They would for yours.

SECOND LADY

Troth, 'tis a doubtful question,
And I'd be loath to put mine to't, my lord.

VORTIGER
Faith, dare you swear for yourselves? It's a plain motion.

SECOND LADY
My lord—

VORTIGER
You cannot deny that with honour,
And since 'tis urg'd, I'll put you to't in troth.

FIRST LADY
May't please your grace—

VORTIGER
'Twill please me wondrous well,
And here's a book; mine never goes without one:
She's an example to you all for purity.
Come, swear, I have sworn you shall, that you never knew
The will of any man besides your husband's.

SECOND LADY
I'll swear, my lord, as far as my remembrance.

VORTIGER
How! Your remembrance! That were strange.

FIRST LADY
Your grace
Hearing our just excuses will not say so.

VORTIGER
Well, what's your just excuse? Y'are ne'er without some.

FIRST LADY
I'm often taken with a sleep, my lord,
The loudest thunder cannot waken me,
Not if a cannon's burthen be discharg'd
Close by mine ear; the more may be my wrong:
There can be no infirmity, my lord,
That's more excusable in any woman.

SECOND LADY
And I'm so troubled with the mother too
I have often call'd in help, I know not whom;
Three at once has been too weak to keep me down.

VORTIGER
I perceive there's no fastening: well fare one then
That ne'er deceives faith's anchor of her hold,
Come at all seasons. [To **CASTIZA**] Here, be thou the star
To guide those erring women, show the way
Which I will make 'em follow. Why dost start,
Draw back, and look so pale?

CASTIZA
My lord—

VORTIGER
Come hither,
Nothing but take that oath; thou'lt take a thousand.
A thousand? Poor! A million, nay, as many
As there be angels' registers of oaths!
Why, look thee, over-holy, fearful chastity,
That sins in nothing but in too much niceness,
I'll begin first and swear for thee myself:
I know thee a perfection so unstain'd,
So sure, so absolute, I will not pant on't
But catch time greedily. By all these blessings
That blows truth into fruitfulness, and those curses
That with their barren breaths blast perjury,
Thou art as pure as sanctity's best shrine
From all man's mixture but what's lawful, mine.

CASTIZA [Aside]
Oh, heaven forgive him, h'as forsworn himself!

VORTIGER
Come,
'Tis but going now my way.

CASTIZA [Aside]
That's bad enough.

VORTIGER
I have clear'd all doubts, you see.

CASTIZA
Good my lord,
Spare me.

VORTIGER
How! It grows later now, then so
For modesty's sake make more speed this way.

CASTIZA
Pardon me, my lord, I cannot.

VORTIGER
What?

CASTIZA
I dare not.

VORTIGER
Fail all confidence
In thy weak kind forever!

DEVONSHIRE
Here's a storm
Able to wake all of our name inhumed
And raise 'em from their sleeps of peace and fame
To set the honour of their bloods right here
Hundred years after; a perpetual motion
Has their true glory been from seed to seed,
And cannot be chok'd now with a poor grain
Of dust and earth. We that remain, my lord,
Her uncle and myself, wood in this tempest,
As ever robb'd man's peace, will undertake
Upon life's deprivation, lands and honour,
She shall accept this oath.

VORTIGER
You do but call me then
Into a world of more despair and horror;
Yet since so wilfully you stand engag'd
In high scorn to be touch'd, with expedition
Perfect your undertakings with your fames,
Or by the issues of abus'd belief
I'll take the forfeit of lives, lands and honours,
And make one ruin serve our joys and yours.

CASTIZA [Aside]
Why, here's a height of misery never reach'd yet;
I lose myself and others.

DEVONSHIRE
You may see
How much we lay in balance with your goodness—
And had we more, it went—for we presume
You cannot be religious and so vild.

CASTIZA
As to forswear myself, 'tis true, my lord,
I will not add a voluntary sin
To a constrain'd one. I confess, great sir,
The honour of your bed has been abus'd—

VORTIGER
Oh, beyond patience!

CASTIZA
Give me hearing, sir:
But far from my consent, I was surpris'd
By villains, and so ravish'd.

VORTIGER
Hear you that, sirs?
Oh, cunning texture to enclose adultery!
Mark but what subtle veil her sin puts on:
Religion brings her to confession first,
Then steps in art to sanctify that lust.
'Tis likely you could be surpris'd.

CASTIZA
My lord!

VORTIGER
I'll hear no more! Our guard, seize on those lords.

DEVONSHIRE
We cannot perish now too fast. Make speed
To swift destruction; he breathes most accursed
That lives so long to see his name die first.

[Exeunt **DEVONSHIRE** and **STAFFORD**, guarded.

HORSUS [Aside]
Ha, ha, here's no dear villainy!

HENGIST
Let him entreat, sir,
That falls in saddest grief for this event,
Which ill begins the fortune of this building,
My lord.

ROXENA [Taking **HORSUS** aside]
What if he should cause me to swear too, captain?
You know, sir, I'm as far to seek in honesty
As the worst here can be; I should be sham'd too.

HORSUS
Why, fool, they swear by that we worship not,
So you may swear your heart out and ne'er hurt yourself.

ROXENA
That was well thought on; I'd quite lost myself.

VORTIGER
You shall prevail in noble suits, my lord,
But this, this shames the speaker.

HORSUS [Aside]
I'll step in now,
Though it shall be to no purpose.—Good my lord,
Think on your noble and most hopeful issue,
Lord Vortimer the prince.

VORTIGER
A bastard, sir!
Oh, that his life were in my fury now!

CASTIZA
That injury stirs my soul to speak the truth
Of his conception. Here I take the book, my lord:
By all the glorified rewards of virtue
And prepared punishments for consents in sin,
A queen's hard sorrow never supply'd a kingdom
With issue more legitimate than Vortimer.

VORTIGER
Pish, this takes not out the stain of present shame though;
To be once good is nothing when it ceases:
Continuance crowns desert; she ne'er can go
For perfect-honest that's not always so.
Beshrew this needless urging of this oath;
'T has justified her somewhat.

HORSUS
To small purpose, sir.

VORTIGER
Amongst so many women not one here
Dare swear a simple chastity? Here's an age
To propagate virtue in! Since I have began't,
I'll shame you all together and so leave you.
My Lord of Kent.

HENGIST
Your highness?

VORTIGER
That's your daughter?

HENGIST
Yes, my good lord.

VORTIGER
Though I'm your guest today,
And should be less austere to you or yours,
In this case pardon me: I will not spare her.

HENGIST
Then her own goodness friend her; here she comes, my lord.

VORTIGER [To **ROXENA**]
The tender reputation of a maid
Makes up your honour, or else nothing can;
The oath you take is not for truth to man,
But to your own white soul, a mighty task.
What dare you do in this?

ROXENA
My lord, as much
As chastity can put a woman to,
I ask no favour; and t' approve the purity
Of what my habit and my time professes,
As also to requite all courteous censure,
Here I take oath I am as free from man
As truth from death, or sanctity from stain.

VORTIGER
Oh, thou treasure that ravishes the possessor!
I know not where to speed so well again;
I'll keep thee while I have thee. Here's a fountain
To spring forth princes and the seeds of kingdoms.
Away with that infection of great honour,
And those her leprous pledges, by her poison
Blemish'd and spotted in their fames forever!
Here we'll restore succession with true peace,
And of pure virgins' grace the poor increase.

[Music. Exeunt all but **HORSUS**.

HORSUS
Ha ha! He's well provided now; here struck my fortune.

With what an impudent confidence she swore honest,
Having the advantage of the oath! The mischiefs
That peoples a lost honour! Oh, they're infinite,
For as at a small breach in town or castle
When one has entrance, a whole army follows,
In woman, so abusively once known,
Thousands of sins has passage made with one:
Vice comes with troops, and they that entertain
A mighty potentate must receive his train.
Methinks I should not hear from fortune next
Under an earldom now. She cannot spend
A night so idly but to make a lord
With ease, methinks, and play. The Earl of Kent
Is calm and smooth, like a deep, dangerous water.
He has some secret way; I know his blood:
The grave's not greedier, nor hell's lord more proud.
Somewhat will hap, for this astonishing choice
Strikes pale the kingdom, at which I rejoice.

[Exit.

DUMB SHOW III

Hoboys. Dumb show. Enter **LUPUS, GERMANUS, DEVONSHIRE, STAFFORD** leading **VORTIMER**; they seat
him in the throne and crown him king. Enter **VORTIGER** in great passion and submission; they neglect
him, then **ROXENA** expressing great fury and discontent. They lead out **VORTIMER** and leave **VORTIGER**
and **ROXENA**; she suborns two **SAXONS** to murder **VORTIMER**; they swear performance and secrecy,
and exeunt with **ROXENA**. Then **VORTIGER** left alone draws his sword and offers to run himself thereon.
Enter **HORSUS** and prevents him; then the **LORDS** enter again and exit **HORSUS**. Then is brought in the
body of **VORTIMER** in a chair, dead; they all in amazement and sorrow take **VORTIGER** and upon his
submission restore him, swearing him against the **SAXONS**. Then enter **HENGIST** with diverse **SAXONS**,
VORTIGER and the rest with their swords drawn threaten their expulsion, whereat **HENGIST**, amaz'd,
sends one to entreat a peaceable parley, which seeming to be granted by laying down their weapons,
exeunt severally.

CHORUS IV

Enter **RAYNULPH**.

RAYNULPH
Of pagan blood a queen being chose,
Roxena hight, the Britons rose,
For[Vortimer they crowned king,
But she soon poisoned that sweet spring.

Then to rule they did restore
Vortiger, and him they swore
Against the Saxons; they, constrain'd,
Begg'd peace treaty, and obtain'd.
And now in numbers equally
Upon the plain near Salisbury,
A peaceful meeting they decreen
Like men of love, no weapon seen.
But Hengist, that ambitious lord,
Full of guile, corrupts his word,
As the sequel too well proves;
On that your eyes, on us your loves.

Exit.

SCENE III - A Plain Near Salisbury

Enter **HENGIST, GENTLEMAN SAXON,** and **SAXONS**.

HENGIST
If we let slip this opportuneful hour,
Take leave of fortune, certainty or thought
Of ever fixing, we are loose at root,
And the least storm may rend us from the bosom
Of this land's hopes forever. But, dear Saxons,
Fasten we now, and our unshaken firmness
Will assure after ages.

GENTLEMAN SAXON
We are resolv'd, my lord.

HENGIST
Observ'd you not how Vortiger the king,
Base in submission, threat'ned our expulsion,
His arm held up against us? Is't not time
To make our best preventions? What should check me?
H'as perfected that great work in our daughter
And made her queen; she can ascend no higher.
Nor can the incessant flow of his love's praises,
Which yet still sways, take from that height it raises;
She's sure enough. What rests then but that I
Make happy mine own hopes, and policy
Forbids no way, noble or treacherous ended:
What best effects is of her best commended.
Therefore be quick, dispatch; here, every man
Receive into the service of his vengeance

An instrument of steel, which will unseen
Lurk like the snake under the innocent shade
Of a spread summer's leaf, and as great substance
Blocks itself up into less room in gold
Than other metals, and less burthensome,
So in the other hand lies all confin'd
Full as much death as ever chang'd mankind.
'Tis all the same time that a small watch shows
As great church dials, and as true as those.
Take heart: the commons love us; those remov'd
That are the nerves, our greatness stands improv'd.

GENTLEMAN SAXON
Give us the word, my lord, and we are perfect.

HENGIST
That's true, the word; I lose myself. Nemp your sexes:
It shall be that.

GENTLEMAN SAXON
Enough, sir, then we strike.

HENGIST
But the king's mine; take heed you touch him not.

GENTLEMAN SAXON
We shall not be at leisure, never fear't;
We shall have work enough of our own, my lord.

[Enter **VORTIGER** and **BRITISH LORDS**.

HENGIST
They come. Calm looks but stormy souls possess you.

VORTIGER
We see you keep your word in all points firm.

HENGIST
No longer may we boast of so much breath
As goes to a word's making, than of care
In the preserving of it when 'tis made.

VORTIGER
Y'are in a virtuous way, my Lord of Kent,
And since w'are both sides well met like sons of peace,
All other arms laid by in sign of favour
If our conditions be embrac'd—

HENGIST
Th'are, th'are.

VORTIGER [Preparing to embrace him]
We'll use no other but these only here.

HENGIST
Nemp your sexes!

[The **SAXONS** seize the **BRITONS**.

BRITISH LORDS
Treason, treason!

HENGIST
Follow to th' heart,
My trusty Saxons, 'tis your liberty,
Your wealth and honour! Soft, y'are mine, my lord.

VORTIGER
Take me not basely, when all sense and strength
Lies bound up in amazement at this treachery.
What devil hath breath'd this everlasting part
Of falsehood into thee?

HENGIST
Let it suffice
I have you and will hold you prisoner,
As fast as death holds your best props in silence.
We know the hard conditions of our peace,
Slavery or diminution, which we hate
With a joint loathing: may all perish thus
That seek to subjugate or lessen us.

VORTIGER
Oh, you strange nooks of guile or subtlety,
Where man so cunningly lies hid from man!
Who could expect such treason from your breast,
Such thunder from your voice? Or take you pride
To imitate the fair uncertainty
Of a bright day, that teems the sudden'st storm,
When the world least expects one? But of all
I'll never trust fair sky in a man again;
There's the deceitful weather. Will you heap
More guilt upon you by detaining me,
Like a cup taken after a full surfeit,
Even in contempt of health and heaven together?
What seek you?

HENGIST
Ransom for your liberty
As I shall like of, or you ne'er obtain 't.

VORTIGER
Here's a most headstrong, dangerous ambition.
Sow you the seeds of your aspiring hopes
In blood and treason, and must I pay for 'em?
Have not I rais'd you to this height?

HENGIST
My lord,
A work of mine own merit, since you enforce it.

VORTIGER
There's even the general thanks of all aspirers:
When they have all the honours kingdoms can impart,
They write above it still their own desert.

HENGIST
I have writ mine true, my lord.

VORTIGER
That's all their sayings.
Have I not rais'd your daughter to a queen?

HENGIST
Why, y'have the harmony of your pleasure for't;
Y'have crown'd your own desires! What's that to me?

VORTIGER
And what will crown yours, sir?

HENGIST
Faith, things of reason:
I demand Kent.

VORTIGER
Why, y'have the earldom on't!

HENGIST
The kingdom on't, I mean, without control,
The full possession.

VORTIGER
This is strange in you.

HENGIST
It seems y'are not acquainted with my blood yet
To call this strange.

VORTIGER
Never was king of Kent yet
But who was general king.

HENGIST
I'll be the first then;
Everything has beginning.

VORTIGER
No less title?

HENGIST
Not if you hope for liberty, my lord.
So dear a happiness would be wrong'd by slighting.

VORTIGER
Well, take 't, I resign 't.

HENGIST
Why, I thank your grace.

VORTIGER
Is your great thirst suffic'd yet?

HENGIST
Faith, my lord,
There's yet behind a pair of teeming sisters,
Norfolk and Suffolk, and I have done with you.

VORTIGER
Y'have got a fearful thirst, my lord, of late,
Howe'er you came by't.

HENGIST
It behooves me then
For my blood's health to seek all means to quench it.

VORTIGER
Them too?

HENGIST
There's nothing will be abated, sir,
Put your assurance in't.

VORTIGER
You have the advantage;
He whom fate captivates must yield to all.
Take 'em.

HENGIST
And you your liberty and peace, my lord,
With our best love and wishes. Here's an hour
Begins us Saxons in wealth, fame and power.

[Exit with all save **VORTIGER**.

VORTIGER
Are these the noblest fruits and fair'st requitals
From works of our own raising?
Methinks the murther of Constantius
Speaks to me in the voice on't, and the wrongs
Of our late queen, slipp'd both into one organ.
Here is no safety for me but what's most doubtful;
The rank rout love me not, and the strength I had
This foul, devouring treachery has demolish'd.

[Enter **HORSUS**.

Ambition, hell, mine own undoing, lust,
And all the brood of plagues conspire against me.
I have not a friend left me.

HORSUS
My lord, he dies
That says it but yourself, were't that thief-king
That has so boldly stol'n his honours from you,
A treason that wrings tears from honest manhood.

VORTIGER
So rich am I now in thy love and pity,
I feel no loss at all; but we must part,
My queen and I, to Cambria.

HORSUS
My lord,
And I not nam'd, that have vow'd lasting service
To life's extremest minute to your fortunes?

VORTIGER
Is my ruin'd fate bless'd with so dear a friend?

HORSUS

My lord, no space in earth nor breadth in sea
Shall divide me from you.

VORTIGER
Oh, faithful treasure!
All my lost happiness is made up in thee.

[Exit.

HORSUS
I'll follow you through the world to cuckold you;
That's my way now. Everyone has his toy
While he lives here: some men delight in building
A trick of Babel and will ne'er be left,
Some in consuming what was rais'd with toiling,
Hengist in getting honour, I in spoiling.

[Exit.

ACT V

SCENE I - A Room in Simon's House

Enter **SIMON**, the clerk **AMINADAB**, **GLOVER**, **FELLMONGER**, **GRAZIER**, etc. as officers. Music.

SIMON
Is not that rebel Oliver, the fustian weaver,
That traitor to my year, 'prehended yet?

AMINADAB
Not yet, so please your worship.

SIMON
Not yet, sayst thou?
How dar'st thou say not yet, and see me present?
Thou malapart clerk that's good for nothing but
To write and read! Is his loom seiz'd on?

AMINADAB
Yes,
And it like your worship, and sixteen yards of fustian.

SIMON
Good; let a yard be sav'd to mend me between the legs, the rest cut in pieces and given to the poor: 'tis heretic fustian, and should be burnt indeed, but being worn threadbare the shame will be as great. How think you, neighbours?

GLOVER
Greater, methinks, the longer it is worn,
Where being once burnt it can be burn'd no more.

SIMON
True, wise and most senseless.

[Enter a **FOOTMAN**.

How now, sirrah?
What's he approaching here in dusty pumps
And greasy hair?

AMINADAB
A footman, sir, to the great King of Kent.

SIMON
The King of Kent? Shake him by the hand for me.
Footman, thou art welcome; lo, my deputy shakes thee:
Come when my year's out and I'll do't myself.
An't were a dog come from the King of Kent,
I keep those officers would shake him, I trow.
And what's the news with thee, thou well-stew'd footman?

FOOTMAN
The king my master—

SIMON
Ha?

FOOTMAN
With a few Saxons
Intends this night to make merry with you.

SIMON
Merry with me? I should be sorry else, fellow,
And take it in evil part, so tell Kent's king.
Why was I chosen mayor but that great men
Should make merry with me? There's a jest indeed;
Tell him I look'd for't, and me much he wrongs
If he forget Simon that cut out his thongs.

FOOTMAN
I'll run with your worship's answer.

[Exit.

SIMON
Do, I prithee.
That fellow will be roasted against supper;
He's half enough already, his brows baste him.
The King of Kent! The king of Kirsendom
Shall not be better welcome to me,
For you must imagine now, neighbours, this is
The time that Kent stands out of Kirsendom,
For he that's king there now was never kirsen'd.
This for your more instruction I thought fit,
That when y'are dead you may teach your children wit.
Clerk!

AMINADAB
At your worship's elbow.

SIMON
I must turn you
From the hall to the kitchen tonight.
Give order that pigs be roasted yellow,
Nine geese, and some three larks for piddling meat,
But twenty woodcocks; I'll bid all my neighbours.
Give charge the mutton come in all blood-raw;
That's infidel meat! The King of Kent's a pagan,
And must be serv'd so. And let those officers
That seldom or never go to church bring 't in,
'Twill be well taken; run.

[Exit **AMINADAB**.

[To an **OFFICER**] Come hither you now.
Take all the cushions down and thwack 'em soundly
After my feast of millers, for their buttocks
Has left a peck of flour in 'em; beat 'em carefully
O'er a bolting-hutch: there'll be enough
For a pan-pudding, as your dame will handle it.
Then put fresh water into both the bough-pots,
And burn a little juniper i' th' hall chimney;
Like a beast as I was, I piss'd out the fire last night
And never thought of the king's coming.

[Enter **AMINADAB**.

How now,
Return'd so quickly?

AMINADAB
Please your worship, there's a certain company of players.

SIMON
Ha, players!

AMINADAB
Country comedians, interluders, sir, desire your worship's leave and favour to enact in the town hall.

SIMON
I' th' town hall? 'Tis ten to one I never grant it. Call 'em before my worship. If my house will not serve their turn, I would fain see the proudest he lend a barn to 'em.

[Enter **CHEATERS**.

Now, sirs, are you comedians?

SECOND CHEATER
We are anything, sir: comedians, tragedians, tragi-comedians, comi-tragedians, pastorists, humourists, clownists, and satirists; we have 'em, sir, from the smile to the laugh, from the laugh to the handkerchief.

SIMON
You are very strong i' th' wrists; and shall these good parts y'are indued withal be cast away upon peddlers and maltmen?

FIRST CHEATER
For want of better company, and't please your worship.

SIMON
What think you of me, my masters? Have you audacity enough to play before so high a person? Will not my countenance daunt you? For if you play before me I shall often look at you; I give you that warning beforehand. Take it not ill, my masters; I shall laugh at you, and truly when I'm least offended with you: my humour 'tis, but be not you abash'd.

FIRST CHEATER
Sir, we have play'd before a lord ere now,
Though we be country actors.

SIMON
A lord? Ha, ha!
You'll find it a harder thing to please a mayor.

FIRST CHEATER
We have a play wherein we use a horse.

SIMON
Fellows, you use no horseplay in my house.
My rooms are rubb'd; keep it for hackney-men.

FIRST CHEATER
We will not offer 't to your worship, sir.

SIMON
Give me a play without a beast, I charge you.

SECOND CHEATER
That's hard. Without a cuckold or a drunkard?

SIMON
Oh, those beasts are often the best men i' th' parish, and must not be kept out! But which is your merriest play now? That I would hearken after.

SECOND CHEATER
Why, your worship shall hear the names all o'er and take your choice.

SIMON
And that's plain dealing, trust me. Come, begin, sir.

SECOND CHEATER
The Whirligig, The Whibble, Carwidgen—

SIMON
Heyday, what names are these?

SECOND CHEATER
New names of late.
The Wild Goose Chase.

SIMON
I understand thee now.

SECOND CHEATER
Gull upon Gull.

SIMON
Why, this is somewhat yet.

SECOND CHEATER
Woodcock of Our Side.

SIMON
Get you further off then.

FIRST CHEATER
The Cheater and the Clown.

SIMON

Is that come up again?
That was a play when I was prentice first.

SECOND CHEATER
Ay, but the cheater has learn'd more tricks since, sir,
And gulls the clown with new additions.

SIMON
Then is your clown a coxcomb? Which is he?

CLOWN
I am the clown, sir.

SIMON
Fie, fie, your company must fall upon him and beat him; he's too fair to make the people laugh.

FIRST CHEATER
Not as he may be dress'd, sir.

SIMON
Faith, dress him how you will, I'll give him that gift he'll never look half scurvily enough. Oh, the clowns that I have seen in my time! The very peeping out of 'em would have made a young heir laugh if his father had lain a-dying; a man undone in law the day before, the saddest case that can be, might for his twopence have burst himself with laughing and ended all his miseries.
Here was a merry world, my masters!
Some talk of things of state, of puling stuff;
There's nothing in a play to a clown's part,
If he have the grace to hit on't, that's the thing indeed:
The king shows well, but he sets off the king,
But not the King of Kent, I mean not so;
The king I mean is one I do not know.

SECOND CHEATER
Your worship speaks with safety, like a rich man,
And for your finding fault, our hope is greater,
Neither with him the clown nor me the cheater.

SIMON
Away then; shift, clown, to thy motley crupper:
We'll see 'em first, the king shall after supper.

[Exeunt **CHEATERS**.

GLOVER
I commend your worship's wisdom in that, Master Mayor.

SIMON

Nay, 'tis a point of justice, an't be well examined, not to offer the king worse than I'll see myself, for a play may be dangerous; I have known a great man poison'd in a play.

GLOVER
What, have you, Master Mayor?

SIMON
But to what purpose many times I know not.

FELLMONGER
Methinks they should destroy one another so.

SIMON
No, no, he that's poison'd is always made privy to it;
That's one good order they have amongst 'em.

[Shout.

What joyful throat is that, Aminadab?
What is the meaning of this cry?

AMINADAB
The rebel is ta'en.

SIMON
Oliver the puritan?

AMINADAB
Oliver, puritan and fustian weaver altogether.

SIMON
Fates, I thank you for this victorious day!
Bonfires of pease-straw burn; let the bells ring.

GLOVER
There's two a-mending, sir, you know they cannot.

SIMON
'Las, the tenor's broken; ring forth the treble.

[Enter **OLIVER** guarded.

I'm overcloy'd with joy! Welcome, thou rebel.

OLIVER
I scorn thy welcome.

SIMON

Art thou yet so stout?
Wilt thou not stoop for grace? Then get thee out.

OLIVER
I was not born to stoop but to my loom;
That seiz'd upon, my stooping days are done.
In plain terms, if thou hast anything to say to me, send me away quickly; this is no biding place. I
understand there's players in the house. Dispatch me, I charge thee, in the name of all the brethren.

SIMON
Nay now, proud rebel, I will make thee stay,
And to thy greater torment see the play.

OLIVER
Oh, devil, I conjure thee by Amsterdam!

SIMON
Our word is past;
Justice may wink a while but see at last.

[A trumpet sounds, and **OLIVER** struggles.

The play begins. Hold, stop him, stop him!

OLIVER
Oh, oh, that profane trumpet!

SIMON
Set him down there, I charge you, officers.

OLIVER
I'll hide mine ears and stop mine eyes.

SIMON
Down with his golls, I charge you!

OLIVER
Oh, tyranny! Revenge it, tribulation!

SIMON
For rebels there are many deaths, but sure the only way
To execute a puritan is seeing of a play.

OLIVER
Oh, I shall swoon!

SIMON
But if thou dost, to fright thee,

A player's boy shall bring thee aqua-vitae.

[Enter **FIRST CHEATER** and **ANOTHER**.

OLIVER
Oh, I'll not swoon at all for't, though I die.

SIMON
Peace, here's a rascal; list and edify.

FIRST CHEATER
I say still he's an ass that cannot live by his wits.

SIMON
What a bold rascal's this! He calls us all asses at first dash; sure none of us lives by our wits, neighbours, unless it be Oliver the puritan.

OLIVER
I scorn as much to live by my wits as the proudest on you all.

SIMON
Why, you are an ass for company, Oliver, and so hold your prating.

[Enter **SECOND CHEATER**.

SECOND CHEATER
Fellows in arms, welcome. The news, the news?

SIMON
Fellows in arms, quoth 'a? He may well call 'em fellows in arms, for they are all out o' th' elbows.

FIRST CHEATER
Be lively, my heart, be lively; the booty's at hand. He's but a fool of a yeoman's eldest son; he comes balanc'd on both sides, bully: he's going to pay rent with th' one pocket, and buy household stuff with th' other.

SECOND CHEATER
And if this be his last day, my chuck, he shall forfeit his lease, quoth th' one pocket, and eat his meat i' th' old wooden platters, quoth th' other.

SIMON
Faith, then he's not so wise as he ought to be if he let such tatterdemalions get th' upper hand on him.

[Enter **CLOWN**.

FIRST CHEATER
He comes, he comes.

SECOND CHEATER
Ay, but do you mark how he comes? Small to our comfort, with both his hands in's pockets. How is't possible to pick a lock when the key's o' th' inside o' th' door?

SIMON
Ay, here's the part now, neighbours, that carries away the play. If the clown miscarry, farewell my hopes forever, the play's spoil'd.

CLOWN
They say there's a foolish thing call'd cheaters abroad that will gull any yeoman's son of his purse and laugh in's face like an Irishman. I would fain meet with one of those cheaters; I'm in as good state to be gull'd now as ever I was in my life, for I have two purses at this time about me, and I'd fain be acquainted with that rascal that would but take one of 'em now.

SIMON
Faith, thou mayst be acquainted with two or three that will do their good wills I warrant you.

FIRST CHEATER
That way's too plain, too easy I'm afraid.

SECOND CHEATER
Come, come, sir, your familiar cheats takes best;
They show like natural things and least suspected:
Give me a round shilling quickly.

FIRST CHEATER
'Twill but fetch one of his hands neither if it take.

SECOND CHEATER
Thou art too covetous. Let's have one at first, prithee;
There's time enough to fetch out th'other after.
[Loudly] Thou liest, 'tis lawful money, current money.

[They draw.

FIRST CHEATER [Loudly]
Ay, so is copper in some countries, sir.

CLOWN
Here's a fray towards, but I'll hold my hands,
Let whose will part 'em.

SECOND CHEATER
Copper! I defy thee,
And now I shall disprove thee. Look you, sir,
Here comes an honest yeoman's son o' th' country,
A man of judgment.

CLOWN
Pray be cover'd, sir;
I have eggs in my cap, and cannot put it off.

FIRST CHEATER
Will you be tried by him?

SECOND CHEATER
I am content, sir.

SIMON
They look rather as if they would be tried next sessions.

FIRST CHEATER
Pray give your judgment of this piece of coin, sir.

CLOWN
Nay, an't be coin you strive about, let's see't;
I love to handle money.

FIRST CHEATER
Look on't well, sir.

[They pick his pocket.

SECOND CHEATER
Let him do his worst, sir.

CLOWN
Y'ad need to wear cut clothes, gentlemen,
Y'are so choleric.

SECOND CHEATER
Nay, rub it and spare't not, sir.

CLOWN
Now by this silver, gentlemen, 'tis good money;
Would y'had a hundred of 'em.

SECOND CHEATER
We hope well, sir.
[Aside to **FIRST CHEATER**]
Th'other pocket now and we are made men.

[Exeunt **CHEATERS**, manet **CLOWN**.

SIMON
Oh, neighbours, I begin to be sick to see

This fool so cozen'd; I would make the case mine own.

CLOWN
Still would I fain meet with this thing call'd cheaters.

SIMON
A whoreson coxcomb! They have met with thee!
I can endure him no longer with patience.

CLOWN
Oh, my rent, my whole year's rent!

SIMON
A murrain on you!
This makes us landlords stay so long
Without our money.

CLOWN
The cheaters have been here!

SIMON
A scurvy hobby-horse, that could not leave his money with me, having such a charge about him! A pox on thee for an ass! Thou play a clown? I will commit thee for offering on't. Officer, away with him.

GLOVER
What means your worship? Why, you'll spoil the play, sir.

SIMON
Before the King of Kent shall be thus serv'd,
I'll play the clown myself. Away with him!

CLOWN
With me? An't please your worship, 'twas my part.

SIMON
But 'twas as foolish a part as ever thou play'd'st in thy life, and I'll make thee smoke for't. I'll teach thee to understand to play a clown, thou shalt know; every man is not born to't. Look thee, away with him quickly,

[Exit **OFFICER** with **CLOWN**.

He'll have the other pocket; I heard him say 't with mine own ears.

[Enter **SECOND CHEATER**.

See, he comes in another disguise to cheat thee again.

SECOND CHEATER [Aside]

Pish, whither goes he now? He spoils all my part.

SIMON
Come on, sir, let's see what your knaveship can do at me now. You must not think now, rascal, you have no fool in hand; I have committed for playing the part so like an ass.

[He throws off his gown, discovering his doublet with a satin forepart and a canvas back.

SECOND CHEATER
What's here to do?

GLOVER
Fie, good sir, come away.
Will your worship base yourself to play a clown?

SIMON
Away, brother, 'tis not good to scorn anything: a man does not know what he may come to; everyone knows his ending but not his beginning. Proceed, varlet, do thy worst, I defy thee!

SECOND CHEATER
I beseech your worship let's have our own clown; I know not how to go forward else.

SIMON
Knave, play out thy part with me or I'll lay thee by the heels all the days of thy life else. Why, how now, my masters, who's that laugh'd now? Cannot a man of worship play the clown a little for his pleasure but he must be laugh'd at? Do you know who I am? Is the king's deputy of no better accompt amongst you? Was I chosen to be laugh'd at? Where's my clerk?

AMINADAB
Here, an't please your worship.

SIMON
Take a note of all those that laugh at me, that when I have done I may commit 'em. Let me see who dares do't now. And now to you once again, sir cheater; look you, here's my purse-strings, I defy thee.

SECOND CHEATER
Good sir, tempt me not; my part is so written that I should cheat your worship and you were my father.

SIMON
I should have much joy to have such a rascal to my son.

SECOND CHEATER
Therefore I beseech your worship pardon me; the part has more knavery than when your worship saw it first. I assure you you'll be deceiv'd in't, sir; the new additions will take any man's purse in Kent or Kirsendom.

SIMON
And thou canst take mine now, I'll give't thee freely,

And do thy worst, I charge thee, as thou'lt answer't.

SECOND CHEATER
I shall offend your worship.

SIMON
Knave, do't quickly!

SECOND CHEATER
Say you so? Then there's for you, and here's for me then.

[Throws meal in his face, takes his purse, and exit.

SIMON
Oh, bless me, neighbours, I am in a fog,
A cheater's fog! I can see nobody!

GLOVER
Run, follow him, officers!

[Exeunt **AMINADAB** and **OFFICERS**.

SIMON
Away, let him go! He'll have all your purses, and he come back. A pox on your new additions! They spoil all the plays that ever they come in; the old way had no such roguery in't, I remember. Call you this a merry comedy, when as a man's eyes are put out? Brother Honeysuckle.

BRAZIER
What says your sweet worship?

SIMON
I make you my deputy to rule the town till I can see again, which I hope will be within nine days at furthest. Nothing grieves me but that I hear Oliver the rebel laugh at me. Pox on your puritan face! This will make you in love with plays ever hereafter; we shall not keep you from 'em now.

OLIVER
In sincerity, I was never better edify'd at an exercise.

SIMON
Neighbours, what colour is the rascal's dust he threw in my face?

GLOVER
'Tis meal, an't please your worship.

SIMON
Meal? I'm glad on't; I'll hang the miller for selling on't.

GLOVER

Nay, ten to one the cheater never bought it;
He stole it certainly.

SIMON
Why, then I'll hang the cheater for stealing on't, and the miller for being out of the way when he did it.

FELLMONGER
Ay, but your worship was in the fault yourself;
You bade him do his worst.

SIMON
His worst? That's true,
But he has done his best, the rascal, for I know not how a villain could put out a man's eyes better, and leave 'em in's head, than he has done.

[Enter the clerk **AMINADAB**.

AMINADAB
Where's my master's worship?

SIMON
How now, Aminadab? I hear thee though I see thee not.

AMINADAB
Y'are sure cozen'd, sir; they are all cheaters professed! They have stol'n three silver spoons too, and the clown took his heels with all celerity; they only take the name of country comedians to abuse simple people with a printed play or two they bought at Canterbury last week for sixpence, and which is worst, they speak but what they list on't and fribble out the rest.

SIMON
Here's no abuse to th' commonwealth,
If a man could see to look into't!
But mark the cunning of these cheating slaves:
First they make justice blind, then play the knaves.

[Enter **HENGIST**.

GLOVER
'Od's precious brother, the King of Kent's new lighted!

SIMON
The King of Kent? Where is he, where is he?
Oh, that I should live to this day, and yet
Not live to see to bid him welcome!

HENGIST
Now where's Simonides, our friendly host?

SIMON
As blind as one that had been fox'd a se'nnight.

HENGIST
Why, how now, man?

SIMON
Faith, practising a clown's part for your grace
I have practis'd both mine eyes out.

HENGIST
What need you practise that?

SIMON
A man's never too old to learn; your grace will say so when you hear all the villainy. The truth 'tis, my lord, I meant to have been merry, and now 'tis my luck to weep water and oatmeal; but I shall see again at supper-time, I make no doubt on't.

HENGIST
This is strange to me, sirs.

[Enter **GENTLEMAN SAXON**.

GENTLEMAN SAXON
Arm, arm, my lord—

HENGIST
What's that?

GENTLEMAN SAXON
With swiftest speed,
If ever you'll behold the queen your daughter
Alive again!

HENGIST
Roxena!

GENTLEMAN SAXON
They're besieg'd,
Aurelius Ambrose and his brother Uther,
With numbers infinite in Britain forces,
Beset their castle, and they cannot 'scape
Without your speedy succour.

HENGIST
For her safety
I'll forget food and rest. Away!

SIMON
I hope
Your grace will hear the jest afore you go.

HENGIST
The jest! Torment me not. Set forward!

SIMON
I'll follow you
To Wales with a dog and a bell, but I'll tell't you.

HENGIST
Unreasonable folly!

[Exit with **GENTLEMAN SAXON**.

SIMON
'Tis sign of war when great ones disagree;
Look to the rebel well till I can see,
And when my sight's recover'd,
I'll have his eyes put out for a fortnight.

OLIVER
Hang thee! Mine eyes! A deadly sin or two
Shall pluck 'em out first, that's my resolution.

[Exeunt **OMNES**.

SCENE II - Before a Castle in Wales]

Enter **AURELIUS** and **UTHER** with **SOLDIERS**.

UTHER
My lord, the castle is so fortify'd—

AURELIUS
So fortify'd? Let wildfire ruin it,
That his destruction may appear to him
I' th' figure of heaven's wrath at the last day,
That murtherer of our brother! Haste away;
I'll send my heart no peace till 't be consum'd.

[**VORTIGER, HORSUS** on the walls.

UTHER
There he appears again; behold, my lord.

AURELIUS
Oh, that the zealous fire on my soul's altar,
To the high birth of virtue consecrated,
Would fit me with a lightning now to blast him
Even as I look upon him!

UTHER
Good my lord,
Your anger is too noble and too precious
To waste itself on guilt so foul as his;
Let ruin work her will.

VORTIGER
Begirt all round?

HORSUS
All, all, my lord, 'tis folly to make doubt on't;
You question things that horror long agone
Resolv'd us on.

VORTIGER
Give me leave, Horsus, though—

HORSUS
Do what you will, sir; question 'em again,
I'll tell 'em over to you.

VORTIGER
Not so, sir;
I will not have 'em told again.

HORSUS
It rests then.

VORTIGER
That's an ill word put in, when thy heart knows
There is no rest at all but torment-making.

HORSUS
True, my heart finds it, that sits weeping blood now
For poor Roxena's safety. You'll confess, my lord,
My love to you has brought me to this danger?
I could have liv'd like Hengist, King of Kent,
And London, York, Lincoln, and Winchester
Under the power of my command, the portion
Of my most just desert; it fell to't, enjoy'd now
By lesser deservers.

VORTIGER

Say you so, sir,
And you'll confess? Since you begin confession,
A thing I should have died before I'd thought on:
I'm out of your love's debt; i' th' same condition,
Y'have marred the fashion of your affection utterly
In your own wicked counsel. There you paid me;
You could not but in conscience love me afterward.
You were bound to do't, as men in honesty
That vitiate virgins to give dowries to 'em:
My faith was pure before to faithful woman.

HORSUS

My lord, my counsel—

VORTIGER

'Tis the map now spread
That shows me all my miseries and discovers
Strange newfound ruin to me; all these objects
That in a dangerous ring circle my safety
Are yours and of your fashioning.

HORSUS

Death mine!
Extremity breeds the wildness of a desert
Into your soul, and since y'have lost your thankfulness,
Which is the noblest part in king or subject:
My counsel do't!

VORTIGER

Why, I'll be judg'd by those
That knit death in their brows, and think me now
Not worthy the acception of a flattery;
Most of those faces smil'd when I smil'd once.
My lords!

UTHER

Reply not, brother.

VORTIGER

Seeds of scorn,
I mind you not; I speak to those alone
Whose force makes yours a power, which else were none.
Show me the main food of your hate, my lords,
Which cannot be the murder of Constantius
That crawls in your revenges, for your love
Was violent long since that.

GENTLEMAN
And had been still,
If from that pagan woman thou'dst slept free;
But when thou fledd'st from heaven, we fled from thee.

VORTIGER [To **HORSUS**]
Was this your counsel now?

HORSUS
Mine? 'Twas the counsel
Of your own lust and blood; your appetite knows it.

VORTIGER
May thunder strike me from these walls, my lords,
And leave me many leagues off from your eyes,
If this be not the man whose Stygian soul
Breath'd forth that counsel to me, and sole plotter
Of all these false, injurious disgraces
That have abus'd the virtuous patience
Of our religious queen.

HORSUS
A devil in madness!

VORTIGER
Upon whose life, I swear, there sticks no stain
But what's most wrongful, and where now she thinks
A rape dwells on her honour, only I
Her ravisher was, and his the policy.

AURELIUS
Inhuman practice!

VORTIGER
Now you know the truth,
Will his death serve your fury?

HORSUS
Mine? My death?

VORTIGER
Will't do't?

HORSUS
What if it would?

VORTIGER

Say, will it do't?

HORSUS
Say they should say it would.

VORTIGER
Why, then it must.

HORSUS
It must?

VORTIGER
It shall; speak but the words, my lord,
He shall be yielded up.

HORSUS
I yielded up?
My lords, believe him not; he cannot do't.

VORTIGER
Cannot?

HORSUS
'Tis but a false and base insinuation
For his own life, and like his late submission.

VORTIGER
Oh, sting to honour, alive or dead thou goest
For that word's rudeness only!

[Stabs him.

GENTLEMAN
See, sin needs
No more destruction than it breeds
In its own bosom.

VORTIGER
Such another brings him.

HORSUS
What, has thy wild rage stamp'd a wound upon me?
I'll send one to thy soul shall never heal for't.

VORTIGER
How, to my soul?

HORSUS

It shall be thy master torment
Both for the pain and the everlastingness.

VORTIGER
Ha, ha!

HORSUS
Dost laugh? Take leave on't; all eternity
Shall never see thee do so much again:
Know thou art a cuckold.

VORTIGER
What!

HORSUS
You change too soon, sir.
Roxena, whom th'ast rais'd to thine own ruin,
She was my whore in Germany.

VORTIGER
Burst me open,
You violence of whirlwinds!

HORSUS
Hear me out first:
For her embrace, which yet my flesh sits warm in,
I was thy friend and follower.

VORTIGER
Deafen me,
Thou most imperious noise that starts the world!

HORSUS
And to serve both our lusts I practis'd with thee
Against thy virtuous queen—

VORTIGER
Bane to all comforts!

HORSUS
Whose faithful sweetness, too precious for thy blood,
I made thee change for love's hypocrisy.

VORTIGER
Insufferable!

HORSUS
Only to make my way to pleasure fearless,

Free and fluent.

VORTIGER
Hell's trump is in that throat!

HORSUS
It shall sound shriller.

VORTIGER
I'll dam it up with death first.

[They stab each other.

I am at thy heart, I hope!

HORSUS
Hold out breath
And I shall find thee quickly.

[**ROXENA** enters in fear.

ROXENA
Oh, for succour!
Who's near me? Help me, save me, the flame follows me!
It's the figure of poor Vortimer the prince,
Whose life I took by poison.

VORTIGER
I'll tug out
Thy soul here.

HORSUS
Do, monster!

ROXENA
Vortiger!

VORTIGER
Monster!

ROXENA
My lord!

VORTIGER
Slave!

ROXENA
Horsus, Horsus!

HORSUS
Murderer!

ROXENA
My lord!

VORTIGER
Toad, pagan!

HORSUS
Viper, Christian!

ROXENA
Hear me, help me!
My love, my lord, I'm scorch'd! What, all in blood?
Oh, happy men, that ebb shows you're near falling.
Have you chose that way yourselves rather to die
By your own swords than feel fire's keener torment
And will not kill me that most needs that pity?
Captain, my lord, send me some speedier death
And one less painful; I have a woman's sufferings.
Oh, think upon't! Go not away so easily
And leave the harder conflict to my weakness.
Most wretched! I'm not worth so much destruction
As would destroy me quickly. And turn back?
I cannot. Oh, 'tis here, my lord, 'tis here!
Horsus, look up, if not to succour me,
To see me yet consum'd. Oh, what is love
When life is not regarded?

VORTIGER
What strength's left
I'll fix upon thy throat.

HORSUS
I have some force yet.

[Both stab, **HORSUS** falls.

ROXENA
No way to 'scape? Is this the end of glory?
Doubly beset with enemy's wrath and fire!
See, for an arm of lust, I'm now embrac'd
With one that will destroy me, where I read
The horror of dishonest actions, guile,
And dissemblance. It comes nearer now, rivers
And fountains fall; tears were now a blessing.

It sucks away my breath; I cannot give
A curse to sin and hear't out while I live.
Oh, help, help, help!

[She falls.

VORTIGER
Burn, burn; now I can tend thee.
Take time with her in torments, call her life
Afar off to thee, dry up her strumpet blood
And hardly parch the skin; let one heat strangle her,
Another fetch her to her sense again,
And the worst pain be only her reviving!
Follow her eternally; give her not o'er
But in a bitter shape. I shall be cold
Before thy rage reach me. Oh, mystical harlot!
Thou hast thy full due, whom lust crown'd queen before
Flames crown her now for a triumphant whore,
And that end crowns 'em all.

[Falls.

AURELIUS
Our peace is full now
In yon usurper's fall, nor have I known
A judgment meet more fearfully.
Here, take this ring, deliver the good queen
And those grave pledges of her injur'd honour,
Her worthy father and her noble uncle,
Too long, too much abus'd, whose clear-ey'd fames
I reverence with respect to holiness due,
A spotless name being sanctity now in few.

[Trumpets sound.

How now, my lords! The meaning of these sounds?

[Enter **DEVONSHIRE, STAFFORD**, leading **HENGIST** prisoner.

HENGIST
The consumer has been here; she's gone, she's lost,
In glowing cinders now lie all my joys!
The headlong fortune of my rash captivity
Strikes not so fierce a wound into my hopes
As thy dear loss.

AURELIUS
Her father and her uncle!

GENTLEMAN
They are indeed, my lord.

AURELIUS
Part of my wishes.
What fortunate power has prevented me
And, ere my love came, brought 'em victory?

GENTLEMAN
My wonder sticks in Hengist, King of Kent.

DEVONSHIRE
My lord, to make that plain which now I see
Fix'd in astonishment: the only name
Of your return and being brought such gladness
To this distracted kingdom, that, to express
A thankfulness to heaven, it grew great
In charitable actions, from which goodness
We tasted liberty that lay engag'd
Upon the innocence of woman's honour,
A kindness that even threat'ned to undo us;
And having newly but enjoy'd the benefit
And fruits of our enlargement, 'twas our happiness
To intercept this monster of ambition,
Bred in these times of usurpation,
The rankness of whose insolence and treason
Grew to such height, 'twas arm'd to bid you battle,
Whom, as our fames' redemption, on our knees
We present captiv'd.

AURELIUS
Had it needed reason
You rightly came provided. What is he?

GENTLEMAN
My lord, that treacherous Hengist, King of Kent.

AURELIUS
I understand not your desert till now, my lords.
Is this that German Saxon whose least thirst
Could not be satisfied under a province?

HENGIST
Had but my fate directed this bold arm
To thy life, the whole kingdom had been mine,
That was my hope's great aim; I have a thirst
Could never have been full quench'd under all:

The whole land must, or nothing.

AURELIUS
A strange drouth!
And what a little ground shall death now teach you
To be content withal!

HENGIST
Why, let it then,
For none else can; y'have nam'd the only way:
When I'm content, it must be when I'm clay.

AURELIUS
My lords, the best requital yet we give you
Is a fair inward joy. Speak to your fames
Glories unblemish'd, for the queen your daughter
Lives firm in honour, neither by consent
Or act of violence stain'd, as her grief judges;
'Twas her own lord abus'd her honest fear,
Whose ends sham'd him, only to make her clear.

DEVONSHIRE
Had your grace given a kingdom for a gift
It had not been so welcome.

[Enter **CASTIZA**, a **GENTLEMAN**.

AURELIUS
Here she comes
Whose virtues I must reverence.

CASTIZA [Kneeling]
Oh, my lord,
I kneel a wretched woman.

AURELIUS [Raising her]
Arise with me,
Great in true joy and honour.

HENGIST
This sight splits me;
It brings Roxena's ruin to my memory.

CASTIZA
My lord, it is too great a joy for life.

AURELIUS
'Tis truth, and that I know you ever joy'd in,

His end confess'd it.

CASTIZA
Are you return'd, soul's comforts?

AURELIUS
Nay, to approve thy pureness to posterity,
The fruitful hopes of a fair, peaceful kingdom
Here will I plant.

CASTIZA
Too worthless are my merits.

AURELIUS
There speaks thy modesty, and to the firmness
Of truth's plantation in this land forever,
Which always groans under some curse without it,
As I begin my rule with the destruction
Of this ambitious pagan, so shall all
With his adulterate faith distain'd and soil'd
Either turn Christians, die, or live exil'd.

OMNES
A blessing on those virtues!

[Flourish. Exeunt.

CHORUS V

Enter **RAYNULPH**.

RAYNULPH
For story of truth compact
I choose these times, these men to act,
As careful now to make you glad
As this were the first day they play'd;
And though some that give none their due
Please to mistake 'em, do not you,
Whose censures have been ever kind:
We hope 'tis good, but if we find
Your grace and love by pleas'd signs understood,
We cease to hope, for then we know 'tis good.

[Exit. Music.

Thomas Middleton was born in London in April 1580 and baptised on 18th April. He was the son of a bricklayer who had raised himself to the status of a gentleman and become the owner of property adjoining the Curtain Theatre in Shoreditch.

Middleton was aged only five when his father died. His mother remarried but this new union unfortunately fell apart and turned into a fifteen year legal conflict centered on the inheritance of Thomas and his younger sister.

Middleton went on to attend Queen's College, Oxford, matriculating in 1598. However he failed to graduate for reasons unknown leaving either in 1600 or 1601. He had by that time written and published three long poems in popular Elizabethan styles. None appears to have been commercially successful although Microcynicon: Six Snarling Satirese was denounced by the Archbishop of Canterbury and publicly burned as part of his attack on verse satire. Although a minor work, the poems show the roots of Middleton's interest in, and later mature work on, sin, hypocrisy, and lust.

In the early years of the 17th century, Middleton made a living writing topical pamphlets, including one, Penniless Parliament of Threadbare Poets, that was reprinted several times as well as becoming the subject of a parliamentary inquiry.

For one so young he was already making quite an impact and had obviously attracted the eye of the authorities in those turbulent times.

Records surviving of the great theatrical entrepreneur of the day, Philip Henslowe, confirm that Middleton was writing for Henslowe's Admiral's Men. His lauded contemporary, a certain William Shakespeare, was writing only for Henslowe whereas Middleton remained a free agent and able to write for whichever theatrical company hired him.

These early years writing plays continued to attract controversy. His friendship and writing partnership with Thomas Dekker brought him into conflict with Ben Jonson and George Chapman in the so-called War of the Theatres. (This controversy was also called the Poetomachia by Thomas Dekker. The Bishops Ban of 1599 had removed any use of satire from prose and verse publications and so the only outlet was on the stage. For the next 3 years Ben Jonson and George Chapman on one side and John Marston, Thomas Dekker and Thomas Middleton on the other poked fun at their opposition with characters from their plays. The grudge against Jonson continued as late as 1626, when Jonson's play The Staple of News indulges in a slur on Middleton's last play, A Game at Chess).

In 1603, Middleton married. It was also a momentous year in other respects. On the death of Elizabeth I, her cousin James VI of Scotland was now also crowned King James I of England. Another outbreak of the plague now forced the theatres in London to close.

For Middleton the changeover from Elizabethan to Jacobean was the beginning of a long period of success as a writer.

When the theatres re-opened and welcomed back audiences in need of entertainment Middleton was there, writing for several different companies. In particular he specialised in city comedy and revenge tragedy.

During this time he appears also to have written with Shakespeare and he is variously attributed as collaborating on All's Well That Ends Well and Timon of Athens.

Although Middleton had started as a junior partner to Thomas Dekker he was now his fully fledged equal. His finest work with Dekker was undoubtedly The Roaring Girl, a biography of the notorious contemporary thief Mary Frith (Frith began her criminal career as a pickpocket before moving on to highway robbery with a penchant for dressing up as a man. A spell in prison was followed by a long career as a 'fence' from her shop in Fleet St. She lived to the then quite extraordinary age of 74.) The writing is noteworthy not only for its playwriting ambition but in producing a fully formed heroine in Moll Cutpurse. This was only shortly after the role of women in plays had seen fit to have them played, in the main, by men.

In the 1610s, Middleton began another playwriting partnership, this time with the actor William Rowley, producing another slew of plays including the classics Wit at Several Weapons and A Fair Quarrel.

The ever adaptable Middleton seemed at ease working with others or by himself. His solo writing credits include the comic masterpiece, A Chaste Maid in Cheapside, in 1613. Interestingly his solo plays are somewhat less thrusting and bellicose. Certainly there is no comedy among them with the satirical depth of Michaelmas Term and no tragedy as raw, striking and as bloodthirsty as The Revenger's Tragedy.

There may be various reasons for this and among them that he was increasingly involved with civic pageants and therefore was trying to avoid too much controversy especially without the cover of a collaborator. Indeed in 1620, he was officially appointed as chronologer of the City of London, a post he held until his death in 1627, when ironically, it passed to his great rival, and sometime enemy, Ben Jonson.

Middleton's official duties did not interrupt his dramatic writing; the 1620s saw the production of his and Rowley's tragedy, and continual favourite, The Changeling, as well as several other tragicomedies.

However in 1624, he reached a peak of notoriety when his dramatic allegory A Game at Chess was staged by the King's Men. The play used the conceit of a chess game to present and satirise the recent intrigues surrounding the Spanish Match; James I's son, Prince Charles, was being positioned to marry the daughter, Maria Anna of the Spanish King Philip IV of Spain. Though Middleton's approach was strongly patriotic, the Privy Council closed the play, after only nine performances at the Globe theatre, having received a complaint from the Spanish ambassador. The Privy Council then opened a prosecution against both authors and actors. Although Middleton in his defence showed that the play had been passed by the Master of the Revels, Sir Henry Herbert, any further performance was forbidden and the author and actors fined.

What happened next is a mystery. It is the last play recorded as having being written by Middleton. His playwriting career appears to have stopped dead. It follows that some sort of further punishment probably occurred and for a writer can there be any greater punishment than not being allowed to write or be heard?

Middleton's work is diverse even by the standards of his age. His career Middleton covers many many genres including tragedy, history and city comedy. As we have noted he did not have the kind of official relationship with a particular company that Shakespeare or Fletcher had that might have supported him in a lean creative period. Instead he appears to have written on a freelance basis for any number of companies. His output ranges from the "snarling" satire of Michaelmas Term, performed by the Children of Paul's, to the bleak intrigues of The Revenger's Tragedy, performed by the King's Men. Interestingly earlier editions of The Revenger's Tragedy attributed the play solely to Cyril Tourneur but recent studies have shredded that view so that Middleton's authorship is not now seriously contested

Indeed modern techniques in analysing writing styles are now leaning towards giving Middleton credit for his adaptation and revision of Shakespeare's Macbeth and Measure for Measure. Along with the more established evidence of collaboration on All's Well That Ends Well and Timon of Athens it appears that Middleton has moved some way forward to the front rank of playwrights and an association, in some form, but its greatest exponent.

His early work was informed by the blossoming, in the late Elizabethan period, of satire, while his maturity was influenced by the ascendancy of Fletcherian tragicomedy. Middleton's later work, in which his satirical fury is tempered and broadened, includes three of his acknowledged masterpieces. A Chaste Maid in Cheapside, produced by the Lady Elizabeth's Men, which skillfully combines London life with an expansive view of the power of love to effect reconciliation even though London seems populated entirely by sinners, in which no social rank goes unsatirised. The Changeling, a later tragedy, returns Middleton to an Italianate setting like that of The Revenger's Tragedy, except that here the central characters are more fully drawn and more compelling as individuals. Similar development can be seen in Women Beware Women.

Middleton's plays are marked by their cynicism, though often very funny, about the human race. His characters are complex. True heroes are a rarity: almost all of his characters are selfish, greedy, and self-absorbed.

When Middleton does portray good people, the characters are often presented as flawless and perfect and given small, undemanding roles. A theological pamphlet attributed to Middleton gives sustenance to the notion that Middleton was a strong believer in Calvinism.

Thomas Middleton died at his home at Newington Butts in Southwark in the summer of 1627, and was buried on July 4th, in St Mary's churchyard which today survives as a public park in Elephant and Castle.

Middleton stands with John Fletcher and Ben Jonson as the most successful and prolific of playwrights from the Jacobean period. Very few Renaissance dramatists would achieve equal success in both comedy and tragedy but Middleton was one. He also wrote many masques and pageants and remains, to this day, one of the most notable of Jacobean dramatists.

Middleton's work has long been praised by many literary critics, among the most fervent were Algernon Charles Swinburne and T. S. Eliot. The latter thought Middleton was second only to Shakespeare.

Among their contemporaries was a very crowded field of talent including: Ben Jonson (1572-1637), Christopher Marlowe (1564-1593), Francis Beaumont (1585-1616), Henry Chettle (1564-1606), John Fletcher (1579–1625), John Ford (1586–1639), John Day (1574-1640), John Marston (1576-1634), John

Webster (1580-1634), Nathan Field (1587-1620), Philip Massinger (1584-1640), Richard Burbage (1567-1619), Robert Greene (1558-1592), Thomas Dekker (1575-1625), Thomas Kyd (1558-1594), William Haughton (died 1605), William Rowley (1585-1626).

It's a daunting list and confirms that to top that made you a very special talent indeed.

Thomas Middleton – A Concise Bibliography

It has long been recognised that the modern concept of authorship was rather more elastic in centuries past. Writers were not only for hire, and their work therefore a commodity, but their plays ran much shorter lengths; two weeks being a common term of performance. To that themes and scenes were liberally excised from one play and used in another. Revisions to past plays that were being restaged would be undertaken and entirely credited to other writers. Many works and plays were unpublished and have not survived and some only from memory by actors etc. Whilst many of these playwrights are only now feted for their talents, some undoubtedly were at the time, but it is difficult to, in every case, to establish exact provenance. With modern scholarly and literary techniques author attributions have sometimes changed or been re-balanced. For those where this may be the case we have placed the *Play's Title and other information* in italics

Plays
Blurt, Master Constable or The Spaniard's Night Walk (with Thomas Dekker (1602)
The Phoenix (1603–4)
The Honest Whore, Part 1, a city comedy (1604), (with Thomas Dekker)
Michaelmas Term, a city comedy, (1604)
All's Well That Ends Well (1604-5); believed by some to be co-written by Middleton based on stylometric analysis.
A Trick to Catch the Old One, a city comedy (1605)
A Mad World, My Masters, a city comedy (1605)
A Yorkshire Tragedy, a one-act tragedy (1605); attributed to Shakespeare on its title page, but stylistic analysis favours Middleton.
Timon of Athens a tragedy (1605–6); stylistic analysis indicates that Middleton may have written this play in collaboration with William Shakespeare.
The Puritan (1606)
The Revenger's Tragedy (1606). Earlier editions often mistakenly attribute authorship to Cyril Tourneur.
Your Five Gallants, a city comedy (1607)
The Family of Love (1607) some attribute this to Middleton others include Dekker and Lording Barry.
The Bloody Banquet (1608–9); co-written with Thomas Dekker.
The Roaring Girl, a city comedy depicting the exploits of Mary Frith (1611); with Thomas Dekker.
No Wit, No Help Like a Woman's, a tragic-comedy (1611)
The Second Maiden's Tragedy, a tragedy (1611); an anonymous manuscript; stylistic analysis indicates Middleton's authorship (though one scholar also attributed it to Shakespeare).
A Chaste Maid in Cheapside, a city comedy (1613)
Wit at Several Weapons, a city comedy (1613); printed as part of the Beaumont and Fletcher Folio, but stylistic analysis indicates comprehensive revision by Middleton & Rowley.
More Dissemblers Besides Women, a tragicomedy (1614)

The Widow (1615–16)
The Witch, a tragicomedy (1616)
A Fair Quarrel, a tragicomedy (1616). Co-written with William Rowley.
The Old Law, a tragicomedy (1618–19). written with William Rowley and perhaps a third collaborator.
Hengist, King of Kent, or The Mayor of Quinborough, a tragedy (1620)
Women Beware Women, a tragedy (1621)
Measure for Measure (1603-4); some scholars argue that the First Folio text was partly revised by Middleton in 1621.
Anything for a Quiet Life, a city comedy (1621). Co-written with John Webster.
The Changeling, a tragedy (1622). Co-written with William Rowley.
The Nice Valour (1622). Printed as part of the Beaumont and Fletcher Folio, but stylistic analysis indicates comprehensive revision by Middleton.
The Spanish Gypsy, a tragicomedy (1623). Believed to be a play by Middleton & Rowley and later revised by Thomas Dekker and John Ford.
A Game at Chess, a political satire (1624). Satirized the negotiations over the proposed marriage of Prince Charles, son of James I of England, with the Spanish princess. Closed after nine performances.

Masques & Entertainments
The Whole Royal and Magnificent Entertainment Given to King James Through the City of London (1603–4). Co-written with Thomas Dekker, Stephen Harrison & Ben Jonson.
The Manner of his Lordship's Entertainment
The Triumphs of Truth
Civitas Amor
The Triumphs of Honour and Industry (1617)
The Masque of Heroes, or, The Inner Temple Masque (1619)
The Triumphs of Love and Antiquity (1619)
The World Tossed at Tennis (1620). Co-written with William Rowley.
Honourable Entertainments (1620–1)
An Invention (1622)
The Sun in Aries (1621)
The Triumphs of Honour and Virtue (1622)
The Triumphs of Integrity with The Triumphs of the Golden Fleece (1623)
The Triumphs of Health and Prosperity (1626)

Poetry
The Wisdom of Solomon Paraphrased (1597)
Microcynicon: Six Snarling Satires (1599)
The Ghost of Lucrece (1600)
Burbage epitaph (1619)
Bolles epitaph (1621)
Duchess of Malfi (commendatory poem) (1623)
St James (1623)
To the King (1624)

Prose

The Penniless Parliament of Threadbare Poets (1601)
News from Gravesend. Co-written with Thomas Dekker (1603)
The Nightingale and the Ant aka Father Hubbard's Tales (1604)
The Meeting of Gallants at an Ordinary (1604). Co-written with Thomas Dekker.
Plato's Cap Cast at the Year 1604 (1604)
The Black Book (1604)
Sir Robert Sherley his Entertainment in Cracovia (1609) (translation).
The Two Gates of Salvation (1609), or The Marriage of the Old and New Testament.
The Owl's Almanac (1618)
The Peacemaker (1618)

Lightning Source UK Ltd.
Milton Keynes UK
UKHW022208220221
379201UK00010B/103

9 781785 438875